A Pra
Mergers, Acqu

A Practical Guide to
Mergers, Acquisitions and Divestitures

Dr Jae K Shim MBA, PHD

Professor of Business
California State University, Long Beach
and
CEO
Delta Consulting Company

GLOBAL
professional
publishing

Global Professional Publishing
Random Acres
Slip Mill Lane
Hawkhurst
Cranbrook
Kent TN18 5AD
Email: publishing@gppbooks.com

ISBN 978-1-906403-75-1

Printed by 4edge

Contents

Preface

Business combinations in the form of mergers and acquisitions of business entities occur when companies choose to combine (rather than grow internally) to take advantage of cost efficiencies or transform their businesses to the next level. The result of a business combination is that the combined company may have additional product offerings, greater geographic presence, increased market share, as well as control over all sources of production and product distribution (vertical integration). Senior staff are frequently called upon to advise management of the impact of proposed combinations, as well as to prepare consolidated financial statements for completed transactions. Knowledge of the emerging accounting rules in this area is critical in supporting both functions.

External growth occurs when a business purchases the existing assets of another entity through a merger. You are often required to appraise the suitability of a potential merger as well as participate in negotiations. Besides the growth aspect, a merger may reduce risk through diversification. The three common ways of joining two or more companies are a merger, consolidation, or a holding company.

Mergers and acquisitions can result in new organizations whose financial and strategic options are much improved. They are driven by globalization, a long-term market, various barriers to growth, which make M&As a valuable tool by which companies can quickly attempt to increase revenue.

This book discusses all facets of mergers and acquisitions (M&As) and divestitures, including deciding on terms, key factors to consider, pros and cons, types of arrangements, evaluative criteria, valuation methods, financial effects of the merger, holding companies, takeover bids, SEC filing requirements, accounting and reporting requirements for business combinations, and financial analysis of combinations. Also addressed is emergence of corporate development officers (CDOs). The appendix includes helpful forms, checklists, and a case study.

Acknowledgments

I wish to express my deep gratitude to Michael Jeffers of Edgewater Editorial Services for this edition. The input and efforts are much recognized and appreciated. Many thanks also go to Allison Shim, a Ph.D. candidate of University of California, Irvine, for her excellent editorial contribution in the production stage.

About the Author

Dr. Jae K. Shim is a professor of business at California State University, Long Beach and CEO of Delta Consulting Company, a financial consulting and training firm. Dr. Shim received his M.B.A. and Ph.D. degrees from the University of California at Berkeley (Haas School of Business). Dr. Shim has been a consultant to commercial and nonprofit organizations for over 30 years.

Dr. Shim has over 50 college and professional books to his credit, including, *Barron's Dictionary of Accounting Terms, Budgeting Basics and Beyond, 2011-2012 Corporate Controller's Handbook of Financial Management, US Master Finance Guide, Project Management, Dictionary of Business Terms, The Vest-Pocket CPA, The Vest-Pocket CFO,* and the best-selling *Vest-Pocket MBA.*

Thirty of his publications have been translated into foreign languages such as Chinese, Spanish, Russian, Polish, Croatian, Italian, Japanese, and Korean. Professor Shim's books have been published by CCH, Barron's, John Wiley, McGraw-Hill, Prentice-Hall, Penguins Portfolio, Thomson Reuters, Global Publishing, American Management Association (Amacom), and the American Institute of CPAs (AICPA).

Dr. Shim has also published numerous articles in professional and academic journals. He was the recipient of the Financial Management Association International's *1982 Credit Research Foundation Award* for his article on cash flow forecasting and financial modeling.

Dr. Shim has been frequently quoted by such media as the *Los Angeles Times, Orange County Register, Business Start-ups, Personal Finance, and Money Radio.* He also provides business content He also provides business content for CPE e-learning providers and for m-learning providers such as iPhone, iPad, iPod Touch, Blackberry, Android, Droid, and Nokia.

CHAPTER 1

Mergers and Acquisitions

For years, academic studies maintained mergers and acquisition (M&A) deals destroyed shareholder value. Nonetheless, market consolidation is set to be high on the agenda in 2012, with delivering cost efficiency through economies of scale being a key driver in the absence of organic growth opportunities, particularly for those companies with a focus primarily on their domestic market. The renewables industry is a niche that could see large numbers of consolidatory M&A deals in the year to come, according to PricewaterhouseCoopers (PwC). M&A in the industry increased by 40 per cent last year and the trend is likely to carry on into 2012. Specifically, this current merger boom is characterized by

▶ Horizontal consolidation with significant potential for cost synergies.
▶ The use by acquirers of existing cash and borrowed money (after-tax cost) to purchase the (relatively higher cost) equity of acquired companies.
▶ Much lower acquisition premiums being initially paid.

Mergers and acquisitions can result in new organizations whose financial and strategic options are much improved. They are driven by globalization, a long-term market, various barriers to growth, which make M&As a valuable tool by which companies can quickly attempt to increase revenue.

This chapter discusses all facets of M&As including deciding on terms, key factors to consider, pros and cons of mergers, types of arrangements, evaluative criteria, valuation methods, financial effects of the merger, holding companies, takeover bids, SEC filing requirements, accounting and reporting requirements for business combinations, and financial analysis of combinations.

External growth occurs when a business purchases the existing assets of another entity through a merger. You are often required to appraise the suitability of a potential merger as well as participate in negotiations. Besides the growth aspect, a merger may reduce risk through diversification. The three common ways of joining two or more companies are a merger, consolidation, or a holding company.

In a merger, two or more companies are combined into one, where only the acquiring company retains its identity. Generally, the larger of the two companies is the acquirer. A merger is a business combination in which the acquiring firm absorbs a second firm, and the acquiring firm remains in business as a combination of the two merged firms. The acquiring firm usually maintains its name and identity. Mergers are legally straightforward because there is usually a single bidder and payment is made primarily with stock. The shareholders of each merging firm involved are required to vote to approve the merger. However, merger of the operations of two firms may ultimately result from an acquisition of stock.

With a consolidation, two or more companies combine to create a new company. None of the consolidation firms legally survive. For example, companies A and B give all their assets, liabilities, and stock to the new company, C, in return for C's stock, bonds, or cash.

A holding company possesses voting control of one or more other companies. The holding company comprises a group of businesses, each operating as a separate entity. By possessing more than 50% of the voting rights through common stock, the holding company has effective control of another company with a smaller percent of ownership.

Depending on the intent of the combination, there are three common ways in which businesses get together so as to obtain advantages in their markets. They are:

- *Vertical merger.* This occurs when a company combines with a supplier or customer. An example is when a wholesaler combines with retailers.
- *Horizontal merger.* This occurs when two companies in a similar business combine. An example is the combining of two airlines.
- *Conglomerate merger.* This occurs when two companies in unrelated industries combine, such as where an electronics company joins with an insurance company.

Mergers

Outstanding planning and execution are essential for a successful merger. Integration is reached only after mapping the process and issues of the companies to be merged. Even then just 23% of all acquisitions earn their cost of capital. When M&A deals are announced, a company's stock price rises only 30% of the time. In acquired companies, 47% of executives leave within the first year, and 75% leave within the first three years. Synergies projected for M&A deals are not achieved 70% of the time. Productivity of merged companies can be affected by up to 50% in the first year and financial performance of newly merged companies is often lacking.

While there is no set formula to guarantee a successful merger, in order to minimize the negative impacts previously discussed, a map of M&A process and issues should be developed. The following steps describe the model of process and issues.

Step 1: Formulate

This stage involves the organization setting out its business objectives and growth strategy in a clear, rational, and data-oriented way. Companies should avoid vague and general objectives. Instead, a specific criteria should be formulated based on the objectives that have been determined and on a strategy of growth through acquisition. These criteria should be expressed in terms of goals like market share, geographic access, new products or technologies, and general amounts for financial synergy. The organization should evaluate the ideal target company based on factors such as the following:

- What type of cost structure does the ideal target have?
- What market channels would this target provide?
- What kinds of organizational competence and capabilities would provide maximum leverage and the greatest number of synergies?
- Are there strategic customer accounts or market segments to be gained?
- In what global regions or countries can we build additional capacity through this target?
- What is the optimum capital structure?
- What are the sources for new acquisitions?
- Will the ideal targets be operated as independent holdings, or does the organization intend to integrate the business partly or fully into its operations?
- If joint venture structures are to be used what level of involvement is desired by the parent company?

Step 2: Locate

After the strategic template has been set in Step 1, the search for desirable target companies should become more focused on financing an operational analysis. These initial parameters, terms, and conditions are defined and ultimately submitted as part of a letter of intent. These letters describe the desired objectives and give an overview of the proposed financial and operational aspects of the transaction. They also include specific details on items like the assets and business units involved, the equity positions of the parent companies, the assumption-of-debt requirements, inter-company supply agreements, employee liabilities, taxes, technology transfer, indemnification, public announcements, and other essential terms and conditions. Additional agreements outside the letter of intent should be made about the following issues. In the case of a joint venture arrangement, the governance structure of the partnership and specific issues for approval need to be agreed upon. The overall process to be used for determining top-level organizational structure and staffing decisions should also be agreed upon. Agreement on the integration process to be used, including mutual participation, formation of key task forces, planning phases, and leadership roles should take place at this point. Another additional agreement that should be made at this point is high-level reconciliation of major discrepancies regarding executive compensation, employee benefits, and incentive compensation plans. Once a consensus is made regarding these agreements, companies can move to Step 3.

Step 3: Investigate

The third step in the model relies on exploring all facets of the target company before finalizing a definitive agreement. Due diligence must be exercised in the financial, operational, legal, environmental, cultural, and strategic areas. Key findings should be summarized for executive review, and all potential merger problems should be identified. Due diligence findings are used to set negotiating parameters, determine bid prices, and provide the basis for initial integration recommendations.

Due diligence is particularly important in light of recent felonious accounting practices. Had Enron or WorldCom been acquired without due diligence, the newly formed company would probably not have uncovered accounting irregularities until months after the acquisition. This could cost billions in market capitalization. There are other areas where due diligence is helpful with assessing risk. The following are key areas to focus due diligence.

▶ **Market.** How large is the target's market? How fast are specific segments growing? Are there threats from substitute technologies or products? To what extent is the market influenced or controlled by governments?

▶ **Customers.** Who are the target's major customers? What are their purchase criteria: price? Quality? Reliability? Do buyers of product X also buy product Y, and do they buy both through similar channels? Are there unmet needs? Are changes in buying behavior to be expected?

▶ **Competitors.** Who are the target's major competitors? What is the degree of rivalry? What are the competitor's strengths and weaknesses? What barriers to entry exist for new competitors? How will the competitors try to exploit the merger or integration issues to their own advantage?

▶ **Culture and human resources.** Which key people must be kept, which core areas of competence should be retained, and how possible is it to do either? Are there major cultural discrepancies with the target? If they could cause major defections or other losses of productivity, is the organization willing to resolve them? If so, at what cost?

To be uninformed on any of these issues can prove to be just as costly as the discovery of fraudulent accounting practices. This level of detailed evaluation must be conducted before an executive team can properly recognize the level of integration that will be appropriate to support the deal.

Exhibit 1 provides a checklist for due diligence.

Exhibit 1: Due Diligence Information to Consider before "Doing a Deal"

Financial

1. Latest audited financial statements.
2. Last unaudited financial statements.
3. Ten-year summary financial statements. (Product P&L essential if more than one product.)
4. Projected operating and financial statements.
5. Full description of securities, indebtedness, investments, and other assets and liabilities other than normal day-to-day accounts.
6. Trial balance and chart of accounts and/or description of accounting practices relative to inventories, fixed assets, reserve accounts, etc.
7. List of bank accounts, average balances.
8. Credit reports from banks and Dun & Bradstreet.
9. Federal income tax status; i.e., tax credits, loss or unused carry forwards, any deficiency claims, etc.
10. Summary of state and local tax situation; i.e., applicable taxes, unemployment tax rate, deficiency claims, etc.
11. Tax status of proposed transaction; recommendation of best method of acquisition.
12. Complete list of insurance policies, including description of coverage and cost: workmen's compensation rate.
13. Statement of responsible officer of business as to unrecorded or contingency liabilities.
14. Statement of inventories.
15. Compare last two physical inventories of sizable money items to reflect slow-moving and obsolete materials. Note finished products particularly. Determine how physical compared with book at last physical inventory.
16. Aged list of accounts receivable, credit and collection policies, and trial balance of accounts payable.
17. Detailed statement of general and administrative expenses, selling expenses, factory overhead on a comparative basis for three years.
18. Status of re-negotiation and price re-determination.
19. Bonus and pension plans; salary and commission contracts.
20. Statement of unfilled orders-present and past.
21. Statistics regarding industry group (trends, return on investment, margin on sales, etc.)

22. If any defense contracts in backlog, check margin of profit. Also, if any existing equipment is government-owned.
23. Statements regarding company's break-even point, including details of product mix, costs, and fixed and variable expenses.
24. Status of production or other contracts requiring company performance for a fixed amount where work is yet to be accomplished.
25. List of outstanding capital-asset items.
26. Status of patents, copyrights, royalty agreements, etc.
27. Details of corporate equity accounts.

Operations

Production

1. Review Estimating Department Procedure and formula used for computing cost to establish sales prices. Also review record of performance versus existing sales prices to determine if all items show a profit. Determine if sales prices are actually based on costs or fixed and influenced by competition without regard to cost.
2. Appraise key production personnel, also constructions and age of buildings, noting those equipped with overhead cranes.
3. Determine if any improvements are planned and authorized, of if any were recently presented and disapproved.
4. Review planning and scheduling procedures.
5. Make casual inspection of property, plant, and equipment and note their condition. Determine age of machinery and if of reputable make.
6. Determine if production employees paid day-work exclusively, or both day-work and piece work, or if some other means of incentive is employed. If other than day-work pay is employed, obtain procedure and any formulas used in establishing the incentive.
7. Determine method of inspection employed.
8. Determine if all power is purchased, manufactured, or combinations of both.
9. Obtain general history of plant growth and rearrangements as far back as possible.
10. Check intrinsic value of patents and (if any) royalty paid on any products or parts produced.
11. Review past overhead charges and obtain explanation of the larger charges.
12. Obtain copies of the following:
    a. Plant plans and flow-charts
    b. Produce list, catalogues, or circulars

   c. Production schedules and forecasts

   d. Labor contracts

   e. Commitments

   f. List of machinery, equipment, fixtures and furniture

   g. Organization chart

   h. Labor utilization reports

   i. Equipment utilization reports

   j. Production reports

   k. Minutes of meetings

   l. Standard cost data

13. Examine union contracts, paying attention to any prior negotiations that are apt to reoccur.

14. Check out labor supply in various geographical areas impacted by company.

Industrial Relations

1. How many employees currently work for the company and what are the employee trends in prior year?

2. What is the labor turnover and what was the labor turnover trend for prior years?"

3. What is the absentee rate?"

4. Is the company unionized? How long? Contracts?

5. What is the labor dispute history?

6. Is the relationship between the company and employees friendly? Between the company and union?

7. Scope of Industrial Relations Department responsibilities

8. What executives participate in negotiations?

9. What procedures exist for:

   a. Hiring

   b. Firing

   c. Promotion

10. What percentage of promotions comes from within?

11. What types of training programs exist? Is there a training department? Training Director?

12. Is there an active safety program?

13. How are pay rates determined?

14. How are fringe benefits determined?

Engineering and Research

1. Description and condition of facilities

2. To whom does the head of the Engineering Department report?

3. Is there a policy manual?
4. What are the short-range and long-range objectives?
5. Obtain department budget.
6. Determine employee turnover.
7. What is the source of engineering employees?
8. Who owns product designs, patents, copyrights, etc.?

Purchasing

1. Make complete analysis of inventory supply.
2. Determine existence of contracts and/or agreements for materials or outside services which are obligations that would have to be assumed.
3. Determine existence of a supplier's equipment or facilities on company property for which responsibility would have to be assumed.
4. Review the details of inventory including the following:
   a. Method, accuracy, and date of prices used
   b. Compare with current prices
   c. Evaluate inventory on basis of what material would bring on an open market
   d. Determine if material is used currently. Make certain that it is not obsolete and/or actually not usable.
5. Review the present employees in the Purchasing Department as to:
   a. Number of employees
   b. Experience
   c. Ability
   d. Personal habits
6. Review the functions of the Purchasing Department including:
   a. Policies
   b. Procedures
   c. Records

Legal

1. Does the seller have power to do the acts the deal requires?
   a. Legal power: SEC, state corporate laws, "Blue Sky" laws, etc.
   b. Corporate power: charter, bylaws, etc.
   c. Contractual power: restriction in bank loan agreements, etc.
2. Does risk exist that seller's shareholders will attack deal as a merger, etc.?
3. Does risk of attack by creditors exist? Review need for compliance with Bulk Sales Act in an asset deal.
4. Is seller's corporation in good standing and qualified in all states in which its business requires same?
5. Is a voting trust needed?

6. If seller was organized within five years, determine names of promoters, nature of an amount of anything of value (including money, property, options, etc.) received or to be received by each promoter directly and indirectly.
7. Is there a material relationship between buyer (or any of its officers and directors) and seller (or any of its officer and directors)?
8. Will seller indemnify buyer against business brokers' and finders' fee?
9. Would the acquisition invite antitrust investigation or prosecution?
10. Are seller's beneficial contracts assignable?
    a. Licenses and royalty agreements
    b. Employment agreements
    c. Leases
    d. Suppliers' contracts
    e. Customers' contracts, particularly U.S. Government
    f. Collective-bargaining agreements
11. Are any of its beneficial contracts already subject to prior assignments - e.g. to lending institutions?
12. Are there customs or contracts which would place an obligation or duty on buyer in either a stock or an asset deal?
    a. Profit sharing plans
    b. Contributory employee stock-purchase or savings plans
    c. Restricted stock-option plans
    d. Pension and bonus plans
    e. Pattern of traditionally high salaries and fringe benefits
    f. Group insurance and similar employee benefit plans
    g. Check also 10a, b, c, d, e, and f
13. Obtain brief description of location and general character of principal plants and officers. If any such property is not owned or is held subject to a major encumbrance, so state and briefly describe how held (consider lease termination dates and powers to renew). Check:
    a. Liens for tax assessments
    b. Liens a/c partial payments, etc. on government contracts
    e. Restrictions, such as zoning, on use of real property and easements
14. Are all required federal and state tax returns filed, examined, and settled?
    a. Income and excess-profits taxes
    b. Franchise and capital stock taxes
    c. Sales and use taxes
    d. Real- and personal-property taxes
    e. Other excise taxes
15. Determine adequacy of all established reserves.

16. Examine re-negotiation procedures, settlements, and reserves.
17. Determine whether contracts with customers have re-determination clauses and minimum net exposure thereunder.
18. Determine whether contracts with suppliers and customers have escalation clauses and maximum net exposure thereunder.
19. How secure are seller's property rights in its:
    a. Patents
    b. Trademarks, trade names, and copyrights
    c. Goodwill
20. Is seller party to any unusual "confidential treatment" or "secret " agreements?
21. Does seller maintain adequate insurance on all insurable property and all reasonable risk? If not, has any significant event occurred with respect to an uninsured property or risk?
22. Review warranties to customers, particularly warranties of design. Determine whether reserves have been established and review history.
23. Does selling company presently have requisite amount of general and specialized legal counsel? Can or should they be continued or changed?
24. Will goodwill or other intangibles result from the transaction? Will the transaction produce the anticipated accounting result? Are any appraisers required?
25. Does seller have benefits under any contracts or other arrangements which would terminate or increase in cost following acquisition?
26. Will transaction result in any minority stockholders, or provide dissenting stockholders with any appraisal rights?

Marketing

1. Description of product line and brief company history.
2. Does the product line of subject company have anything in common with the lines produced by existing divisions of the buyer?
3. Ten-year record of the company's product sales performance and methods of distribution.
4. What reputation does the company enjoy among its customers?
5. Check the consistency of production covering the last three to five years for seasonal trends or diminishing demand for any products.
6. Long-range forecast of growth or contraction trends for this industry. What are the prospects of substitute materials, processes, or products?
7. Who are the customers? What is the long-range outlook for the future business of these customers?

8. Three- to five-year forecast of demand for the product, and estimate of industry's ability to supply.
9. An evaluation of the company's three- to five-year forecast of sales expectations (share of market).
10. Present competitors:
    a. Description of competitive products
    b. Location and size of plants
    c. Share of market
    d. Pricing policies
    e. Methods of distribution
    f. Reputation and financial details
11. Analysis of past price trends and policies and present or future pricing policies for the production line, considering:
    a. Competitive pricing
    b. Cost pricing
12. Analysis of present and potential customers:
    a. Major types of customers and percentage of sales to each
    b. Geographical location
    c. Buying habits
13. Analysis-location of plant:
    a. Competitive accessibility to major markets
    b. Distribution costs
14. Review and evaluate Sales Department:
    a. Sales management
    b. Organization and operating procedures
    c. Field sales force-compensation, turnover rate, sales training
    d. Sales policies
15. Review and evaluate advertising and promotion programs and policies:
    a. Objectives and techniques of the advertising program
    b. Analysis of principal elements of advertising budget
    c. Appraisal of advertising organization, personnel, and agency relationships
    d. Comparison of techniques and program with those of major competitors

Organization

1. Does the company have an organization chart?
    a. Is it maintained currently?
    b. Does it properly reflect the assigned functions?

2. Does the company have an organization manual which maintains organization charts and job descriptions?
    a. Is it maintained up to date?
    b. Do the job specifications properly reflect the jurisdiction, authority, and responsibility of the job?
3. Does the company have a policy manual containing the president's policy statements and the written interpretations of policy issued by the officers, executives, and general management?
4. Is there a program which is actively pursued to train and develop outstanding employees for management and executive positions?
5. Is there a program of individual executive ratings on an annual basis? If so, review the ratings pertaining to key personnel.
6. Does the company maintain an education program for its employees?
    a. What are the annual costs?
    b. What percentage of the employees participates in the program?
7. Does the company maintain a scholarship program? What are the annual costs?
8. Review the salary rates of key personnel.

Public Relations

1. Does the company have a Public Relations Department? Is it properly staffed? To whom does the public relations director, or the person responsible for the function, report?
2. Does the company have a planned public relations program? Does the program encompass the major public, including:
    a. Press
    b. Stockholders
    c. Financial community
    d. Plant communities
    e. Employees
    f. Customers
3. How does the above-mentioned public consider the company?
4. Does the company have an institutional advertising campaign?
5. Does the company employ outside public relations consultants?
6. Will the acquisition of the company be a public relations asset to the buyer?

Step 4: Negotiate

This step includes requirements for successfully reaching a definitive agreement. Deal teams should be briefed by due diligence teams, who together with executives should formulate the final negotiating strategy for all terms and conditions of the deal. Considerations include price, performance, people, legal protection, and governance.

Step 5: Integrate

The last step of the model should be customized to each organization and adapted to each specific deal. This is the actual process of planning and implementing the newly formed organization with its processes, people, technology, and systems. In determining how to resolve the issues that arise at this stage, the merging organizations must carefully consider such questions as how fast to integrate, how much disruption will be created, how disruption can be minimized, how people can be helped to continue focusing on customers, safety, and day-to-day operations, and how to best communicate with all the stakeholder groups of the company.

Exhibit 2 outlines the previously discussed Watson Wyatt Deal Flow and the processes and issues involved.

Exhibit 2: Map of M&A Processes and Mergers

	Formulate	Locate	Investigate	Negotiate	Integrate
	• Set business strategy	• Identify target markets and companies	• Due diligence analysis	• Set deal terms:	• Finalize and execute integration plans:
	• Set growth strategy	• Select target	1. Financial 2. People/Culture 3. Legal 4. Environmental 5. Operational 6. Capitals	1. Legal 2. Structural 3. Financial • Secure key talent and integration teams	1. Organization 2. Process 3. People 4. Systems
Key Activities	• Define acquisition criteria • Begin strategy implement- ation	• Issue letter of Intent • Develop M&A Plan • Offer letter of confidentiality	• Finding summary • Set preliminary integration plans • Decide negotiation parameters	• Close deal	

	Formulate	Locate	Investigate	Negotiate	Integrate
Issues	• Costs	• ROI/Value	• Liabilities	• Price	• Speed
Risks	• Channels	• Strategic Fit	• Human Capital	• Performance	• Disruption
	• Content	• Cultural Fit	• retention/ eliminate	• People	• Costs
	• Competencies	• Timing		• Protection	• Revenues
	• Customers	• Leadership Fit	• Financial Viability	• Governance	• Results
	• Countries	• Potential synergy	• Integration Issues		• Perception:
	• Capital	• Viability	• Synergies		1. Share-holders
	• Capacity		• Economy of scale		2. Public
					3. Customers
			• ROI		4. Employees

Pros and Cons of a Merger

There are many reasons why your company may prefer external growth through mergers instead of internal growth.

Advantages of a Merger

▶ Increases corporate power and improves market share and product lines.

▶ Aids in diversification, such as reducing cyclical and operational effects.

▶ Helps the company's ability to raise financing when it merges with another entity having significant liquid assets and low debt.

▶ Provides a good return on investment when the market value of the acquired business is significantly less than its replacement cost. Studies suggest that the shareholders of target firms that are acquired receive the greatest benefit.

▶ Improves the market price of stock in some cases, resulting in a higher P/E ratio. For example, the stock of a larger company may be viewed as more marketable, secure, and stable.

▶ Provides a missed attribute; that is, a company gains something it lacked. For instance, superior management quality or research capability may be obtained.

▶ Aids the company in financing an acquisition that would not otherwise be possible to obtain, such as where acquiring a company by exchanging stock is less costly than building new capital facilities, which would require an enormous cash outlay. For instance, a company may be unable to finance significant internal expansion but can achieve it by purchasing a business already possessing such capital facilities.

▶ Achieves a synergistic effect, which means that the results of the combination are greater than the sum of the parts. For instance, greater profit may result from the combined entity that would occur from each individual company due to increased efficiency (e.g., economies of scale)and cost savings (e.g., eliminating overlapping administrative functions, volume discounts on purchases). There is better use of people and resources. A greater probability of synergy exists with a horizontal merger since duplicate facilities are eliminated. *Operational synergy* arises because the combined firm may be able to increase its revenues and reduce its costs. For example, the new firm created by a horizontal merger may have a more balanced product line and a stronger distribution system. Furthermore, costs may be decreased because of economies of scale in production, marketing, purchasing, and management. *Financial synergy* may also result from the combination. The cost of capital for both firms may be decreased because the cost of issuing both debt and equity securities is lower for larger firms. Moreover, uncorrelated cash flow streams will provide for increased liquidity and a lower probability of bankruptcy. Still another benefit is the availability of additional internal capital. The acquired company is often able to exploit new investment opportunities because the acquiring company has excess cash flows. *Note:* Synergy equals the value of the combined firm minus the sum of the values of the separate firms. These values can be calculated using the capital budgeting technique of discounted cash flow analysis. The difference between the cash flows of the combined firm and the sum of the cash flows of the separate firms is discounted at the appropriate rate, usually the cost of equity of the acquired firm. The components of the incremental cash flows are the incremental revenues, costs, taxes, and capital needs.

▶ Obtains a tax loss carryforward benefit if the acquired company has been losing money. The acquirer may utilize the tax loss carryforward benefit to offset its own profitability, thus reducing its taxes. Note, however, that Section 382 of the IRC sets the limit as to how much net operation losses an organization that has just undergone an ownership change can deduct from its income. The maximum deductible amount is derived by multiplying the value of the old loss corporation's stock prior to the change in ownership by the long term tax exempt rate. It's usually 4-7% of the actual loss that is able to be utilized.

▶ Use surplus cash from a tax perspective. Dividends received by individual shareholders are fully taxable, whereas the capital gains from a combination are not taxed until the shares are sold. In addition, amounts remitted from the acquired to the acquiring firm are not taxable. The combined firm's capital structure also may allow for increased use of debt financing, which results in tax savings from greater interest reductions.

Disadvantages of a Merger

▶ Reverse synergies which reduce the net value of the combined entity (e.g., adjustments of pay scales, costs of servicing acquisition debt, defections of key acquired company staff).

▶ Adverse financial effects because the anticipated benefits did not materialize; for example, expected cost reductions were not forthcoming.

▶ Antitrust action delaying or preventing the proposed merger.

▶ Problems caused by dissenting minority stockholders.

Note: A proxy fight is an attempt by dissident shareholders to gain control of the corporation, or at least gain influence, by electing directors. A proxy is a power of attorney given by a shareholder that authorizes the holder to exercise the voting rights of the shareholder. The proxy is limited in its duration, usually for a specific occasion like the annual shareholders' meeting. The issuer of a proxy statement must file a copy with SEC ten days prior to mailing it to shareholders all material information concerning the issues. A form that indicates the shareholder's agreement or disagreement must be provided. Also, if the purpose is for voting for directors, proxies must be accompanied by an annual report.

In evaluating a potential merger, you have to consider its possible effect upon the financial performance of the company, including:

▶ *Earnings per share.* The merger should result in higher earnings or improved stability.

▶ *Dividends per share.* The dividends before and after the merger should be maintained to stabilize the market price of the stock.

▶ *Market price of stock.* The market price of the stock should be higher or at least the same after the merger.

▶ *Risk.* The merged business should have less financial and operating risk than before.

A merger of two companies may be achieved in one of two ways. The acquirer may negotiate with the management of the prospective acquired company, which is the preferred approach. If negotiations are not successful, the acquirer may make a tender offer directly to the stockholders of the targeted company. A *tender offer* represents a cash offer for the common shares held by stockholders. The offer is made at a premium above the current market price of the stock. In some cases, the tender may be shares in the acquiring company rather than cash. Minority shareholders are not required to tender their shares. Consequently, not all of the target firm's stock is usually tendered. Usually an expiration date exists for the tender.

Note:

1. Corporate takeover specialists prefer tender offers because proxy fights can be prolonged by target firm management. With less time to organize a

defense, target management is less effective than when they contest proxy fights.

2. A good takeover candidate includes a cash-rich business, a company with a low debt-to-equity ratio, and a company with significant growth potential.
3. In a two-tier offer, better terms are offered to shareholders who sell early. For example, early sellers may receive cash and late sellers, bonds.
4. Leverage buyout (LBO) is used as a defensive tactic against a hostile takeover by tender offer. A leveraged buyout (LBO) entails the company going private. A small group of investors, usually including senior management purchases the publicly owned shares. The shares will then be delisted because they will no longer be traded. Thus, an LBO competes with a hostile tender offer as alternative.

In discussions with management, the acquirer typically makes a stock offer at a specified exchange ratio. The merger may take place if the acquired company receives an offer at an acceptable premium over the current market price of stock. Sometimes contingent payments are also given, such as stock warrants.

There are several financing packages that buyers may use for mergers, such as common stock, preferred stock, convertible bonds, debt, cash, and warrants. A key factor in selecting the final package is its impact on current earnings per share (EPS).

If common stock is exchanged, the seller's stock is given in exchange for the buyer's stock, resulting in a tax-free exchange. The drawback is that the stock issuance lowers earnings per share because the buyer's outstanding shares are increased. When there is an exchange of cash for common stock, the selling company's stockholders receive cash, resulting in a taxable transaction. This type of exchange may increase EPS since the buying company is obtaining new earnings without increasing outstanding shares.

Guidelines

In an effort to provide guidelines as to what type of business combinations would and would not be challenged in antitrust actions, the Justice Department developed the Herfindahl-Hirshman Index. It essentially breaks all business combinations into the three broad types: horizontal integration, vertical integration, and conglomeration.

Market Share Squared	Likelihood of Challenge
Less than 1,000	Unlikely
1,000 – 1,800	Possible
More than 1,800	Likely

Consider this hypothetical market share breakdown in the widget industry:

Widget Industry Market Share Data		
	Market Share	Market Share Squared
Company A	41%	1,681
Company B	26%	676
Company C	18%	324
Company D	8%	64
Company E	5%	25
Company F	2%	4

Note: The Federal Trade Commission (FTC), in conjunction with the antitrust division of the Justice Department, has broad authority to enforce the antitrust laws. Since mergers may lessen competition or tend to create a monopoly under the terms of the Clayton Act, they are scrutinized by the FTC and the Justice Department.

What does this mean?

It is obvious that Company A cannot combine with either Company B or C, but how about Company E? Company A would be prohibited from combining with any other company. Combining the market shares of Company A and any other company and then squaring them would produce a number higher than 1,800.

Wrong Calculation

	Market Share	Market Share Squared
Company A	41%	1,681
Company F	2%	4
		1,685

Note: Do not make this mistake unless you are hungry for attention by the antitrust division of the Justice Department.)

Correct Calculation

	Market Share	Market Share Squared
Company A	41%	
Company F	2%	
	43%	1,849

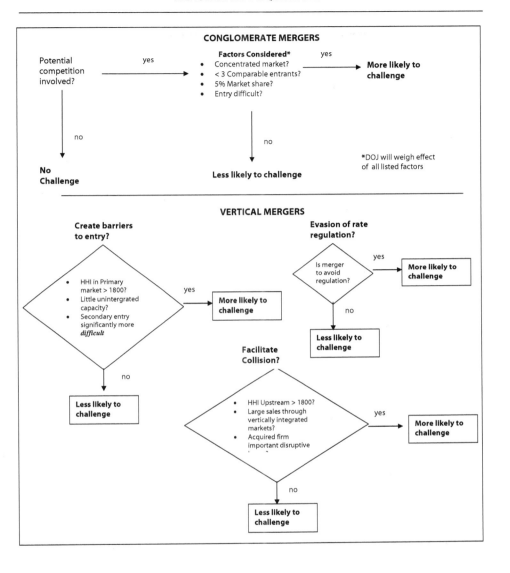

CONGLOMERATE MERGERS

Potential competition involved? — yes →

Factors Considered*
- Concentrated market?
- < 3 Comparable entrants?
- 5% Market share?
- Entry difficult?

yes → **More likely to challenge**

no ↓

no ↓

No Challenge

Less likely to challenge

*DOJ will weigh effect of all listed factors

VERTICAL MERGERS

Create barriers to entry?

- HHI in Primary market > 1800?
- Little unintergrated capacity?
- Secondary entry significantly more *difficult*

yes → **More likely to challenge**

no ↓

Less likely to challenge

Evasion of rate regulation?

Is merger to avoid regulation? — yes → **More likely to challenge**

no ↓

Less likely to challenge

Facilitate Collision?

- HHI Upstream > 1800?
- Large sales through vertically integrated markets?
- Acquired firm important disruptive

yes → **More likely to challenge**

no ↓

Less likely to challenge

Horizontal Mergers

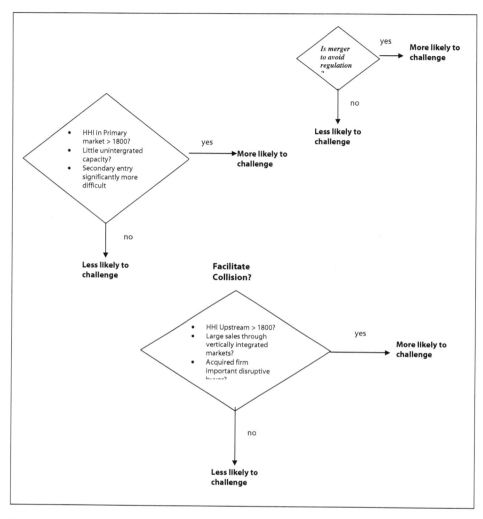

The following summarizes M&A percent rules.

M & A Percent Rules

100%	Absolute control of company
80%	Threshold for tax-free deals
50% + 1 share	Control, but minority interests may cause heartburn
15% - 25%	When stock is widely-held (no big blocks held by individuals)

| 15 to 25 percent | provides effective control over the company. This is generally true because in a proxy battle, management and stockholders would each obtain about 50 percent of the uncommitted shares. |
| 5% | Threshold when public must be notified of the purchaser's intent. |

Planning for Mergers and Acquisitions

Perhaps the most striking aspect of corporate mergers and acquisitions is the seemingly random dispersion of the successes and failures among such combinations. For every well-publicized case of "one plus one equals more than two" there seems to be another (albeit less well publicized) in which one plus one equals, if not exactly zero, at any rate substantially less than two.

Obviously some mergers are good, and others are fatal. It would be naive to assert that the good mergers are always the result of effective planning and the careful study of facts, while the fatal ones are invariably the result of management by inspiration. Experience does suggest, however, that there is more than a chance relationship between planning and success in corporate combinations. Smart management takes the time and effort to study each prospective combination in such detail as is necessary to permit a well-thought out decision. Such a study invariably begins with a clear understanding of just what it is that the company hopes to achieve through the combination in question.

Defining Objectives

Why are there such things as corporate mergers and acquisitions? At the risk of oversimplification, it might be helpful if we arranged some of the more common reasons for business combinations into a few broad categories:

1. *Market considerations.* One frequent merger objective is to capture a greater share of the market which the company serves. A merger may make it possible for the company to offer a complete product line for the first time, or it may expand the geographic area in which the company sells its goods. Foreign acquisitions are frequently made for this latter reason.

2. *Distribution economies.* Often a single distribution system (including salesmen, jobbers, dealers, retail outlets, and, of course, transportation facilities) can handle two products having common, or at least similar, markets *and* distribution methods at a lower unit cost than it can a single product.

3. *Diversification.* Many companies embark on merger programs to avoid the cyclical effect of a single industry, to minimize the impact of adverse conditions in a particular market, and/or to be able to participate in new growth areas.

4. *Manufacturing advantages.* By combining two manufacturing units, weaknesses can often be strengthened, overcapacity eliminated, and over-head reduced. Seasonal problems, particularly, can often be solved in this way.

5. *Research and development needs.* R&D cost is becoming an increasingly important element of overhead in almost every field of business and industry. Common laboratories and other R&D facilities frequently result in a reduction in research cost per unit of production.

6. *Financial considerations.* The purpose of a merger is often to secure higher earnings per share and an improved image in the marketplace and consequently a higher price/earnings ratio or to achieve greater financial security and stability.

7. *Redeployment of excess capital.* Many insurance companies have millions of dollars in low-yield securities in excess of their reserve requirements.

8. *Personnel considerations.* This is most commonly a motive of service organizations. Frequently a merger is undertaken to provide key personnel for an organization weakened through death or through failure to plan ahead for orderly management succession.

9. *Complexity and automation.* The business world is becoming increasingly complex. A small enterprise unable to support a staff of specialists or to afford the cost savings available to larger entities through automation may seek refuge in a merger with a larger operation. Similarly, two small companies, neither of which is able to afford these necessities, may join to create an organization of sufficient size to cope with the growing complexity of business life and to compete with larger operations.

A review of these considerations will at least serve to start management thinking in an orderly, logical way about the possibility of merger. Could your company benefit in any of the areas outlined above? If so, you have the beginning of a merger plan. This plan must be carefully developed by top management until the specific objectives of your merger program are clearly defined and understood.

Defining Criteria

A major product of the acquisition planning process is the definition of detailed acquisition criteria for each area where acquisition appears to be a viable alternative to internal growth. A list of criteria should resemble a purchase order, describing the most desirable candidate imaginable. A typical list would include such factors as the following:

- Industry or industry segment
- Method of distribution
- Size
- Geographic constraints
- Particular strengths
- Importance of management continuation
- Preferred consideration (cash or stock)
- Maximum price

Admittedly, it is unlikely that a willing and available dream candidate will be identified, but it is important to create a benchmark against which to evaluate candidates. Weighting the importance of each characteristic, either formally or informally, also aids in the candidate-screening process and in ranking candidates in order of attractiveness.

Finding and Screening Candidates

The next step is to find companies that will fit the overall plan. Is the secrecy of the plan important? if so, the problem of finding available companies becomes considerably more difficult. Most managements under these circumstances have found that secrecy is a relative term. The old cynic's saw, that two can keep a secret if one of them is dead, has a great deal of support among those who have been involved in mergers. In most cases the best approach is to throw open the doors and cry in the marketplace that you are interested in a purchase or merger. In practice this can be accomplished simply by passing the word, either personally or by advertisement, to your business friends, lawyers, brokers, and bankers that you are associated with.

It is generally desirable to establish two or three benchmarks against which to measure prospective acquisitions to decide whether they are worth pursuing further. Since this is a first rough screening, the criteria should be as objective as possible, and capable of simple application on the basis of readily available data. Some illustrative benchmarks are:

- A price/earnings ratio not more than 10 percent higher than ours; or
- A growth rate for the last five years of 12 percent per annum, compounded annually.

Your first screening will, of course, let through some bad deals. More seriously, the application of any arbitrary criteria is likely to eliminate some desirable deals. But where there is a large number of a choice, an arbitrary method of elimination is better than none at all.

The process of identifying prospective acquisition candidates begins with building a universal list of all companies that appear to meet the criteria. Multiple sources should be consulted. Easily accessible electronic databases generally can provide 80 to 90 percent of the names with some amount of additional information. Other sources of candidate information include the following:

▶ Trade association membership lists
▶ Trade publications
▶ Industry experts
▶ Government publications
▶ Acquirer's employees—purchasing, sales, and so on
▶ Public library

Naturally, the law of diminishing returns applies to the last few names, but more than 95 percent of the qualified candidates that exist can be identified easily.

Screening several hundred companies to identify the most attractive candidates sounds like a difficult and time-consuming task. Actually, applying unequivocal knockout criteria such as size or location quickly reduces the number of companies to a manageable number. Comparing the remainder against the other criteria should produce ten or fifteen priority candidates. The task of gathering comprehensive information regarding that smaller number of candidates is not nearly as formidable.

The prospect identification process also gives the acquirer a feel for the dynamics of the targeted industry. Competitive conditions, industry growth trends, profit margins, and other important data can easily be gathered at the same time. Analyzing the characteristics that distinguish high-performing industry participants is also a useful exercise.

Once the internal process is complete, it is important to turn to external sources of prospective candidates— financial intermediaries. Typically, an investment banker or broker is present in about two thirds of all merger transactions. Contact with intermediaries should be established to get an early look at as many opportunities as possible—to be plugged into the "deal flow."

Deciding on Acquisition Terms

In deciding on acquisition terms, consideration should be given to the following:

▶ Earnings in terms of absolute dollars and percentage change
▶ Dividends
▶ Market price of stock
▶ Book value per share
▶ Net working capital per share

The weight assigned to each of the above varies with the circumstances involved.

Earnings

In determining the value of earnings in a merger, you should take into account anticipated future earnings and projected P/E ratio. A rapidly growing company is expected to have a higher P/E multiple.

Dividends

Dividends are attractive to stockholders. However, the more a company's growth rate and earnings, the less is the impact of dividends on market price of stock. On the other hand, if earnings are falling, the effect of dividends on per share is greater.

Market Price of Stock

The price of a security considers projected earnings and dividends. The value assigned to the company in the acquisition will most likely be greater than the present market price in the following instances:

▶ The business is in a depressed industry.
▶ The acquired company is of greater value to the acquirer than to the stock market in general.
▶ A higher market price than the current one is offered to induce existing stockholders to give up their shares.

Book Value per Share

Since book value is based on historical cost rather than current value, it is not a key factor to consider. However, when book value exceeds market value, there may be an expectation that market price will increase subsequent to the merger due to improved circumstances (e.g., superior management).

Net Working Capital per Share

If the acquired company has very low debt or very liquid assets, the acquirer may borrow the funds for the acquisition by using the acquired company's strong liquidity position.

Grading Criteria

In acquisition strategy, document what a firm wants to accomplish by the acquisition and how the acquisition will complement the company's overall strategy. Industries and companies are then screened by employing various quantitative measures and considering qualitative factors. The broad industry sectors should be narrowed down by comparing each industry to specified industry criteria. The industry best satisfying set goals is then selected. After the target industry has been identified, companies in that industry are then screened. Make sure to compare the target's trend to industry averages to determine the company's relative position.

In identifying an acquisition target, clearly defined criteria should be established for acceptable candidates, all companies within the category should be reviewed, suitable companies should be listed in priority order, and a short list of targets (generally no more than 10) coming closest to the ideal profile should be prepared. This short list can either consist of the highest-scoring companies regardless of score or all companies. The profile criteria include what is important to you, such as industry classification, size, profitability, leverage, market share, and geographic area. You may not be able to get your first choice, so flexibility is needed.

Different criteria should have different weights depending upon importance to you. For example, the weight may go from 1 (least important) to 10 (most important). For example, you may decide to assign a 1 to dividend history and a 10 to industry. Most criteria will fall between 1 and 10 (e.g., leverage may be assigned a weight of 2 because all candidates have already been screened to have a debt-to-equity ratio below 25%). Intermediate attributes within a range may also be scored. For example, revenues under $100 million or above $300 million may be given a score of 4. An illustrative grading guide follows.

Illustrative Grading Guide

Industry Classification

1	=	specialty shops, diversified companies in which food products retailing is only minor
10	=	convenience store chain

Size

1	=	revenues under $10 million or over $40 million
10	=	revenues of $30 million

Fixed Assets (book value)

1	=	$2 million
10	=	over $5 million

Net Income

1	=	profit margin below 2%
5	=	profit margin above 10%

Leverage

1	=	over 40% debt-to-equity ratio
10	=	below 5% debt-to-equity ratio

Geographics

1	=	West
5	=	South
10	=	Northeast

You can save time by using a computer database to find possible target companies. The database enables you to select ranges for size, profitability, leverage, and so on and then screen out candidates fulfilling your requirements. Information on publicly held companies is much more available than for closely held businesses.

Factors in Determining a Price

There are many factors to be considered in determining the price to be paid for a business including:

- ▶ Financial health of the acquired company (e.g., quality of earnings, growth rate, realizability of assets)
- ▶ Type and stability of operations
- ▶ Maturity of business
- ▶ Degree of competition
- ▶ Tax consequences, such as unused tax credits
- ▶ Expected return on assets and sales
- ▶ Employee relations, such as the absence of unionization
- ▶ Risk level, such as having adequate insurance
- ▶ Corporate characteristics, including having negatively correlated product lines, and favorable lease terms
- ▶ Management quality, such as experienced executives
- ▶ Marketing position, such as quality product line, market share, distribution channels, and customer base
- ▶ Economic environment, including recession-resistant business
- ▶ Political environment, such as the absence of strict governmental regulation and operations in politically unstable areas
- ▶ Structure of the arrangement, including debt or equity, cash or stock, costs of the transaction, and time period
- ▶ Improvement in diversification and/or integration
- ▶ Ease of transferability of ownership
- ▶ Exchange rate fluctuations

- Legal issues, such as the possibility of stockholder liability suits
- Industry characteristics, such as being in a growing industry instead of a declining one
- Impact of the acquisition on the acquiring company's financial strength and operation performance.
- Possible violation of antitrust laws. These laws are administered by the Department of Justice's Antitrust Division and the Federal Trade Commission.

When looking at the targeted company, review both the positive and negative effects. Proper assessment can be made on what to pay for the candidate by examining what will happen after the merger. If the analysis includes many uncertain factors, sensitivity analysis may be used to look at the effect of changes in outcome.

Be Careful: Detailed financial planning and analysis are required in the acquisition process. If an acquiring company overpays for a target company, this negatively affects its financial position. Many of the deals behind some of the record corporate write-offs of the past few years (e.g., 2011-2012) can be characterized as acquirers paying too much to buy faster-growing companies that they may - or may not - have been well positioned to manage and integrate.

Acquisition Strategy and Process

A brochure should be prepared by the buyer so the target company may be acquainted with the buyer's objectives, philosophy, and background. A proposal should also be prepared explaining to the target company the financial and operating benefits of a merger.

Planning to integrate the acquired company into the buyer should take place early in the acquisition process. Areas requiring planning include policies and procedures, data processing, organizational and management structure, personnel, operations, financial reporting, customer base, and supplier relationships.

After discussions become serious, the investigation of the target company should involve reviewing available financial information and audit work papers, tax returns, visiting the target's facilities, and interviewing management (e.g., research and development programs, manufacturing and distribution methods). There should be a purchase audit, particularly to "key" accounts and exposure areas to uncover problems and issues not fully disclosed in the financial statements. For example, inventory should be observed and counted and a determination made whether their valuation in the financial records is appropriate. The purchase audit must consider financial, accounting, and operating matters. Outside consultants may need to be retained in specialized areas (e.g., technology, product capability).

The areas of investigation include:

▶ Industry (e.g., competition, growth rate, governmental regulation, barriers to entry).

▶ Target company background and history (e.g., nature of business, locations and facilities, lawsuits, environmental considerations).

▶ Financial and accounting information (e.g., ratios by major business segment, effect of inflation or recession on company, current values). The financial statements for the last three years should be reviewed.

▶ Taxes (e.g., tax attributes of target, tax-planning strategies). Tax returns should be reviewed and analyzed for the last three years. Financial income and taxable income should be reconciled. Does the state penalize multi-state enterprises? Will foreign countries impose significant tax burdens? What tax benefits will the purchase accomplish (e.g., available tax credits)? Are there any questionable items or limitations that may be challenged by the tax authorities?

▶ Management quality (particularly important when moving into an unrelated industry).

▶ Pension and health care obligations.

▶ Marketing (e.g., backlog, new product developments, obsolescence problems).

▶ Manufacturing (e.g., production facilities, manufacturing processes and efficiencies).

▶ Distribution network, facilities, and methods.

▶ R&D experience.

Financing of the Merger

The range of possible transaction structures is infinite, but the following are some of the basic alternatives:

▶ All cash transaction, financed from existing cash resources
▶ All cash transaction, financed by issuing stock
▶ Stock transaction, merger through exchange of stock
▶ Mixed stock/cash
▶ Leveraged cash transaction, financed through debt issue
▶ Leveraged buyout, majority of equity replaced by debt
▶ Debt transaction, debt offered to selling company shareholders
▶ Mixed cash/debt
▶ Preferred stock

Should stock or assets (generally cash) be given in the acquisition?

Advantages of Giving Stock

▶ No cash or financing requirement for acquirer.
▶ Quick and simple in terms of document preparation. There is a transfer of stock certificates in exchange for immediate or deferred payment.
▶ In certain cases, stock transactions can be exempt from taxation to shareholders, thus potentially raising the value of the transaction.
▶ A stock acquisition can maintain the equity-to-assets ratio, and even provide additional capital for further growth strategies.
▶ Target shareholders share risk of acquisition.
▶ Minority stockholders may not have appraisal rights.
▶ Typically, stockholder votes authorizing the purchase or sale are not required.
▶ May take advantage of acquirer's high stock price.
▶ Target management has incentive to maintain commitment.

Disadvantages of Giving Stock

▶ Can be less attractive to target shareholders.
▶ The acquirer, in buying stock of the target company, assumes its liabilities, whether disclosed or not.
▶ Dilution of acquirer shareholder earnings.
▶ Dilution of ownership/control.
▶ Risk of conflict after merger.
▶ If the target is liquidated subsequent to acquisition, much work is needed in conveying the target company's assets as part of the liquidation.

Advantages of Giving Assets

▶ Acquirer has complete control over the assets it buys and the liabilities it assumes.
▶ Attractive to shareholders because they value immediately and have no risk.
▶ Typically, no acquiring company stockholder vote is needed.
▶ Easier to understand.

Disadvantages of Giving Assets

▶ Dilution of earnings.
▶ Difficult to determine the fair value of each asset.
▶ Current target management may have little incentive to facilitate transaction or maintain commitment after transaction.
▶ Target company's stockholders must approve.

► State transfer taxes must be paid.
► A cash acquisition can materially lower the equity to assets ratio of the surviving company.
► Creditor agreement may be needed for certain transfers and assignments.
► Must conform to bulk sales laws.

If the decision is made to give cash to the targeted company shareholders, some form of equity and/or debt will have to be issued because it is unusual for the acquiring company to have sufficient cash or liquid assets to finance the entire transaction. Debt financing may range from an intermediate-term loan for part of the purchase price to structural debt financing of 90% or more of the price (leveraged buyout). There are many considerations in deciding whether to use leverage and in determining the appropriate amount of leverage.

Advantages of Leverage
► Interest expense is tax deductible.
► Increased return to shareholders.
► Since shareholders' ownership is maintained, there is a lack of dilution.

Disadvantages of Leverage
► Creditors have priority claim on merged company.
► The greater financing risk may lower the company's stock and bond prices as well as result in increasing costs of financing.
► Possible lowering in credit standing and bond ratings.
► A cash problem may result in default.
► Interest payments lower earnings.
► Interest and principal payments reduce cash flow.

Leveraged buyouts are quite popular. A leveraged buyout occurs when an entity primarily borrows money (sometimes 90% or more) in order to buy another company. Typically, the acquiring company uses as collateral the assets of the acquired business. Generally, repayments of the debt will be made from the yearly operating funds flow of the acquired company. A leveraged buyout may also be made when the acquiring company uses its own assets as security for the loan. It may also be used if a firm wishes to go private. In most cases, the stockholders of the acquired company will receive an amount greater than the current price of the stock. A leveraged buyout involves more risk than an acquisition done through the issuance of equity securities.

The high debt service requirement drains cash flow during the period that the debt is outstanding. However, once debt is retired, shareholders enjoy ownership of the remaining enterprise. The debt may be reduced rapidly by selling some assets or divisions of the acquired company, if warranted.

The characteristics conducive to a leveraged buyout are:

▶ The earnings and cash flow of the company must be predictable so they may cover interest and principal payments on the debt financing.

▶ The growth rate of the firm should exceed the inflation rate.

▶ There must be a good market share and product line otherwise the firm is vulnerable to an economic decline or competitive actions.

▶ There should be a good asset base to serve as collateral.

▶ The assets should not be presently encumbered and the debt-equity ratio should currently be low.

▶ There are minimal capital expenditure requirements.

▶ The company should be liquid so that it has enough cash to meet its debt obligations.

▶ There is future salability of the company, if desired.

▶ Technological change is not a problem.

▶ Management is highly qualified and is given a significant equity stake.

▶ The business is selling at a low P/E ratio.

Preferred Stock Financing

One important development in 2001 is the disappearance of the pooling-of-interests merger-accounting method, which required the use of common stock. Now, companies must employ purchase accounting, regardless of payment terms. And stock offers no advantage in purchase accounting. This is a method with which the purchasing company treats the target firm as an investment, adding the target's assets to its own fair market value. If the amount paid for a company is greater than fair market value, the difference is reflected as *goodwill*.

Preferred stock is one tool companies may now employ more frequently in financing their acquisitions. Like corporate bonds, preferred shares offer investors a predictable income stream, in the form of dividends that must be paid before any distributions to common shareholders. While those preferred dividends can't be deducted for tax purposes, as interest payments on debt are, preferred shares offer the same equity relief for stressed corporate balance sheets that common stock does.

A big advantage of equity is its ability to preserve a transaction's tax-free status for selling shareholders. For an acquisition to qualify as a tax-free reorganization, sellers must maintain a "continuity of interest" in the new business. That's usually accomplished by a common share swap, but preferred shares can also do the trick.

The Use of Capital Budgeting Techniques in Appraising the Acquisition

In deciding whether to buy another business, capital budgeting may be used. Also, the effect of the new capital structure on the firm's overall cost of capital has to be projected.

Example 1

W Company is contemplating purchasing P Company for $95,000. W's current cost of capital is 12%. P's estimated overall cost of capital after the acquisition is 10%. Projected cash inflows from years one through eight are $13,000. (Assume no residual value.)

The net present value is:

Year	Present Value
0 (-$95,000 x 1)	($95,000)
1-8 ($13,000 x 5.3349)	+ 69,354*
Net present value	($25,646)

* Using 10% as the discount rate, from Table 2 (Present value of an annuity of $1).

The acquisition is not feasible since there is a negative net present value.

Example 2

C Company wants to buy some fixed assets of B Company. However, the latter wants to sell out its business. The balance sheet of B Company follows:

Assets	
Cash	$ 4,000
Accounts receivable	8,000
Inventory	10,000
Equipment 1	16,000
Equipment 2	28,000
Equipment 3	42,000
Building	110,000
Total assets	$218,000

Liabilities and Stockholders' Equity	
Total liabilities	80,000
Total equity	138,000
Total liabilities and equity	$218,000

C wants only equipment 1 and 2 and the building. The other assets excluding cash, can be sold for $24,000. The total cash received is thus $28,000 ($24,000 + $4,000 initial cash balance). B desired $50,000 for the whole business. C will thus have to pay a total of $130,000 which is $80,000 in total liabilities and $50,000 for its owners. The actual net cash outlay is therefore $102,000 ($130,000 - $28,000). It is expected that the after-tax cash inflows from the new equipment will be $27,000 per year for the next five years. The cost of capital is 8%. (Assume no residual value.)

The net present value of the acquisition is:

Year	**Present Value**
0 (-$102,000 x 1)	($102,000)
1-8 ($27,000 x 3.9927)	107,803
Net present value	$5,803

Since there is a positive net present value the acquisition should be made.

Exchange Ratio

T Company buys B Company. T Company's stock sells for $75 per share while B's stock sells for $45. As per the merger terms, T offers $50 per share. The exchange ratio is 0.667 ($50/$75). Thus, T exchanges 0.667 shares of its stock for one share of B.

Effect of Merger on Earnings per Share and Market Price per Share

A merger can have a positive or negative impact on net income and market price per share of common stock.

Example 3

Relevant information follows:

	Company A	**Company B**
Net income	$50,000	$84,000
Outstanding shares	5,000	12,000
EPS	$10	$7
P/E ratio	7	10
Market price	$70	$70

Company B acquires Company A and exchanges its shares for A's shares on a one-for-one basis. The effect on EPS follows:

	B Shares Owned after Merger	**EPS before Merger**	**EPS after Merger**
A stockholders	5,000	$10	$7.88*
B stockholders	12,000	7	7.88*
Total	$17,000		

* Total net income is determined as:

5,000 shares x $10	$50,000
12,000 shares x $7	84,000
	$134,000

$$EPS = \frac{Net\ income}{Total\ shares} = \frac{\$134,000}{17,000} = \underline{\$7.88}$$

EPS decreases by $2.12 for A stockholders and increases by $0.88 for B stockholders.

The effect on market price is not clear. Assuming the combined entity has the same P/E ratio as Company B, the market price per share will be $78.80 (10 x $7.88). The stockholders experience a higher market value per share. The increased market value occurs because net income of the combined entity is valued at a P/E ratio of 10, the same as Company B, while before the merger Company A had a lower P/E multiplier of 7. However, if the combined entity is valued at the lower P/E multiplier of 7, the same as Company A, the market value would be $55.16 (7 x $7.88). In this case, the stockholders in each firm experience a reduction in market value of $14.84 ($70.00 - $55.16).

Since the effect of the merger on market value per share is not clear, the crucial consideration is EPS.

Example 4

The following situation exists:

Market price per share of acquiring company	$100
Market price per share of acquired company	$20
Price per share offered	$24

The exchange ratio equals:

Shares	$24/$100	0.24
Market price	$24/$20	1.2

Example 5

M Company wants to buy J Company by issuing its shares. Relevant information follows:

	M Company	J Company
Net income	$40,000	$26,000
Outstanding shares	20,000	8,000

The exchange ratio is 2 to 1. The EPS based on the original shares of each company follows:

EPS of combined equity = Combined net income/Total shares

			EPS
$\dfrac{66000}{20,000 + (8,000 \times 2)}$	=	$\dfrac{66000}{36,000 \text{ shares}}$	=1.83
EPS of M	=	$1.83	
EPS of J	=	$1.83 × 2	= $3.66

Example 6

O Company wants to buy P Company by exchanging a 1.8 shares of its stock for each share of Company P. Company O expects to have the same P/E ratio after the merger as before. Applicable data follows:

	O Company	P Company
Net income	$500,000	$150,000
Shares	225,000	30,000
Market price per share	$50	$60

The exchange ratio of market price equals:

$$\frac{\text{Offer price}}{\text{Market price of P}} \qquad \frac{\$50 \times 1.8}{\$60} = \frac{90}{\$60} = 1.5$$

EPS and P/E ratios for each company follow.

	O Company		P Company	
EPS	$500,000/225,000	= $2.22	$150,000/30,000	= $5
P/E Ratio	$50/$2.22	=22.5	$60/$5	= 12

The P/E ratio used in obtaining P is:

$$\frac{1.8 \times \$50}{\$5} = \frac{\$90}{\$5} = 18 \text{ times}$$

The EPS of O after the acquisition is:

$$\frac{650000}{225,000 + (30,000 \times 1.8)} = \frac{\$650,000}{279,000 \text{ shares}} = \$2.33$$

The expected market price per share of the combined entity is:
2.33×22.5 times = $52.43

Risk of the Acquisition

In appraising the risk associated with an acquisition, a scenario analysis may be used looking at the best case, worst case, and most likely case. Operating scenarios consider assumptions as to variables including sales, volume, cost, competitive reaction, governmental interference, and customer perception. You derive the probability for each scenario on the basis of experience. Sensitivity analysis may be used to indicate how sensitive the project's returns are to variances from expected values of essential variables. For example, you may undertake a sensitivity analysis on selling prices assuming they are, for example, 10% to 15% higher or lower than expected. The theory behind sensitivity analysis is to adjust key variables from their expected values in the most likely case. The analysis can be performed assuming one purchase price or all possible purchase prices. What is the effect, for example, of a 4% change in the gross profit rate on projected returns?

Based on sensitivity analysis, you should pay an amount for a target company resulting in cutoff return given the most likely operating scenario.

Warning: It is difficult to accomplish successful unrelated diversification. This was the case with General Electric and its Insurance Solutions division. The Insurance Solutions division had few connections with the core business of its parent and had been underperforming for years, so at the end of 2005, GE sold it to Swiss Re.

Recommendation: Acquisition of companies operating in related fields usually has a higher success rate.

Holding Company

A holding company is one whose sole purpose is to own the stock of other companies. To obtain voting control of a business, the holding company may make a direct market purchase or tender offer. A company may elect to become a holding company if its basic business is declining and it decides to liquidate its assets and use the funds to invest in growth companies.

Since the operating companies owned by the holding company are separate legal entities, the obligations of one are isolated from the others.

Recommendation: A loan officer lending to one company should attempt to obtain a guarantee by the other companies.

Advantages of a Holding Company

▶ Risk protection, in that the failure of one company does not cause the failure of another or of the holding company. If the owned company fails, the loss of the holding company is restricted to its investment in it.
▶ Ability to obtain a significant amount of assets with a small investment. The holding company can control more assets than it could acquire through a merger.
▶ Ease of obtaining control of another company; all that is needed is to purchase enough stock in the marketplace. Unlike a merger which requires stockholder or management approval, no approval is needed for a holding company.

Disadvantages of a Holding Company

▶ More costly to administer than a single company resulting from a merger because economies of scale are not achieved.
▶ Incurrence of increased debt because the acquisition may magnify variability in earnings, thus subjecting the holding company to more risk.
▶ The chance that the U.S. Department of Justice will deem the holding company a monopoly and force dissolution of some of the owned companies.
▶ Multiple taxes because the income the holding company receives is in the form of cash. Before paying dividends, the subsidiary must pay taxes on the earnings. When profit is distributed to the holding company as dividends, it must pay tax on the dividends received less an 80% or more of

the subsidiary's shares, a 100% dividend exemption exists. No multiple tax exists for a subsidiary that is part of a merged company.

Example 7

A holding company owns 70% of another firm. Dividends received are $20,000. The tax rate is 34%. The tax paid on the dividend follows:

Dividend	$20,000
Dividend exclusion (80%)	16,000
Dividend subject to tax	4,000
Tax rate	x 34%
Tax	$1,360

The effective tax rate is 6.8% ($1,360/$20,000).

Hostile Takeover Bids

If a negotiated takeover of another company is impossible, a hostile bid may be needed. In a hostile bid, management of the targeted company is bypassed, and the stockholders are approached directly. The acquirer argues that management is not maximizing the potential of the company and is not protecting the interest of shareholders.

In a tender offer, the buyer goes directly to the stockholders of the target business to tender (sell) their shares, typically for cash. The tender in some cases may be shares in the acquiring company rather than cash. If the buyer obtains enough stock, it can gain control of the target company and force the merger. Cash rather than securities is usually used because a stock offering requires a prospectus thereby losing the advantages of timeliness and surprise. Stockholders are induced to sell when the tender price substantially exceeds the current market price of the target company stock. Typically, there is an expiration date to tender.

Hostile takeovers are typically quite costly because they usually involve a significant price incentive, and antitakeover measures. They can be disruptive to both buyer and seller because of "slur" campaigns. It is rare that smooth transitions of management take place.

The typical features of a hostile takeover candidate may include:

1. A multidivisional organization that has diverse business activities.
2. Asset values of component divisions are not reflected in the market price of the company's stock.
3. Financial performance of the individual business lines could be better.
4. Existing management is unable to realize the true value of the company.

The usual initial step in launching a hostile bid is to buy stock of the target company in the open market. The SEC requires that any investor who buys more than a 5% interest in a public company should register his or her holding and provide the intent (e.g., passive or to gain eventual control) through a Schedule 13-D filing. Beyond 5% ownership, it becomes difficult to make open-market purchases of stock without revealing the intention to acquire control (except that acquirers may accumulate a greater holding within the five days allowed for the 13-D filing, or they may elect to make a passive investment for a limited period before reassessing the intention to acquire control.) The acquiring business must furnish to the management of the potential acquired company and to the SEC 30 days notice of its intent to acquire. Once the intention to acquire control is made public, the stock price of the target company generally rises in expectation of a tender offer at a higher price.

The direct appeal to shareholders, which often follows is frequently made through a public tender offer. Management of the target company will typically recommend that shareholders reject the offer and will possibly propose an alternative restructuring arrangement.

The management of a targeted company can fight the takeover attempt in the following ways:

1. Purchase treasury stock to make fewer shares available for tendering.
2. Initiate legal action to prevent the takeover, such as by applying antitrust laws.
3. Postpone the tender offer (some states have laws to delay the tender offer).
4. Declare an attractive dividend to keep stockholders happy.

Advantages of a Hostile Bid

▶ Direct communication with stockholders to bypass management intransigency.
▶ Flexibility to alter terms.
▶ Increased value of existing stake.
▶ Improved profitability of the target.

Disadvantages of a Hostile Bid

▶ Price: hostile bidders may pay a high premium especially if competition arises in the takeover attempt.
▶ Cost: high transaction and advisory costs.
▶ Risk: hostile bids often fail.
▶ Creation of ill will and problems with integrating the target after merger.
▶ Possible adverse litigation or regulatory action.
▶ Possible retaliatory action by target.

SEC Filing Requirements

When an acquisition of a significant business occurs, the buyer and, where appropriate, the target company must file a Form 8-K (filing for important events), a proxy or information statement (if shareholders must vote), and a registration statement (if securities are to be issued). Significant business means the acquirer's investment in the target exceeds 10% of its consolidated assets. In addition, certain information on the acquisition must be presented in Form 10-Q (quarterly filing).

If a significant business has been acquired, a Form 8-K must be filed within 15 days containing information about the acquisition and including historical financial statements and pro forma data.

If the combination must be voted upon by shareholders of any of the companies, a Form S-4 must be filed. In other cases, one of the other S forms must be filed.

If Form S-4 is filed, there is a 20-business-day waiting period between the date the prospectus is sent to stockholders and the date of the stockholder meeting. Also, if the acquisition must be voted upon by shareholders of one or both of the companies, a proxy or information statement must be furnished to shareholders and filed with the SEC.

Regulation S-X requires audited historical financial statements of a business to be acquired. The financial statements must be for the last three years and any interim period. In a purchase combination, there must be a pro forma statement of income for the most recent year and interim period.

Tax Considerations

The tax effect of a transaction may require an adjustment in selling price. It may be desirable to have an "open-end" arrangement, whereby with the attainment of a given sales volume or profit, additional stock will be issued by the purchaser to the selling company or its stockholders ---so handled to be nontaxable.

The acquiring company should prefer a taxable transaction. In a taxable transaction, the acquiring company must allocate its purchase cost among the assets acquired based on the present values of those assets. Any residual balance is goodwill. The acquired company's net assets will typically have a book value far below their fair market value. A taxable transaction allows the acquiring company to step up the tax basis of these assets, sometimes to a level even higher than original cost, and to start the depreciation stepped-up basis will reduce the taxable gain on the sale.

Defensive Measures by Targeted Company

The targeted company may have in place preventive measures against being taken over including:

1. *Golden Parachute.* Management compensation arrangements that are triggered when there is a purchase of the business such as lump-sum benefits, employment agreements, and stock options. Examples are Greyhound and Hughes Tool.

2. *Poison Pill.* When a hostile bid is eminent, the targeted company takes out significant debt (or issues preferred stock) that makes the company unattractive to the hostile acquirer because of the high debt position. A poison pill may be included in a target corporation's charter, by-laws, or contracts to reduce its value to potential tender offerors. A poison pill may be, for example, a right granted to the target firm's shareholders to purchase shares of the merged firm resulting from a takeover. The bidding company loses money on its shares because this right dilutes the value of its stock. Examples are Union Carbide and CBS, Inc.

3. *Self-Tender.* After a hostile bid, the target company itself makes a counteroffer for its own shares. An example is Newmont Mining.

4. *Greenmail.* The target company buys back the stock accumulated by the raider, at a premium. Examples are Texaco, Walt Disney, and Goodyear.

5. PAC-MAN. The defending company makes a counteroffer for the stock of the raiding company. Examples are American Brands and Bendix Corporation.

6. *White Knight.* The defending company finds a third party who is willing to pay a higher premium, typically with "friendlier" intentions than the raider. Examples are Gulf Oil Corp. (Chevron) and Sterling Drugs (Eastman Kodak).

7. *Asset Spinoff.* The defending party identifies the assets most desirable to the raider. It then spins off the assets to one of its separate companies or sells them to a third party. Examples are Union Carbide and Marathon Oil.

The Valuation of a Targeted Company

In a merger, we have to value the targeted company. As a starting point in valuation, the key financial data must be accumulated and analyzed including historical financial statement, forecasted financial statements, and tax returns. The assumption of the valuation must be clearly spelled out.

The valuation approaches may be profit- or asset-oriented. Adjusted earnings may be capitalized at an appropriate multiple. Future adjusted cash earnings may be discounted by the rate of return that may be earned. Assets may be valued at fair market value, such as through appraisal. Comparative software programs are available to do merger analysis.

Comparison with Industry Averages

Valid comparisons can be made between the entity being valued and others in the same industry. Industry norms should be noted. General sources of comparative industry data found financial advisory services include Standard and Poor's, Moody's, Value Line, Dun and Bradstreet and Robert Morris Associates. Trade publications may also be consulted. Reference may be made to the *Almanac of Business and Industrial Financial Ratios* (based on corporate tax returns to the Internal Revenue Service) written by Leo Troy and published by Prentice Hall. If a small company is being acquired, reference may be made to *Financial Studies of the Small Business* published annually by Financial Research Associates (Washington,D.C. :Financial Research Associates, 1984).

Publicly available information on the targeted company include the annual report; SEC Forms 10-K, 10-Q, and 8-K; interim shareholder reports; proxy statements; press releases; and offering prospectuses.

We now look at the various approaches to business valuation consisting of capitalization of earnings, capitalization of excess earnings, capitalization of cash flow, present value (discounted) of future cash flows, book value of net assets, tangible net worth, economic net worth, fair market value of net assets, gross revenue multiplier, profit margin/capitalization rate, price earnings factor, comparative value of similar going concerns, and recent sales of stock. A combination of approaches may be used to obtain a representative value.

Capitalization of Earnings

Primary consideration should be given to earnings when valuing a company. Historical earnings are typically the beginning point in applying a capitalization method to most business valuations. In general, historical earnings are a reliable predictor of future earnings. According to IRS Revenue Ruling 59-90, 1959-1, C.B.237, the greatest emphasis should be placed on profitability when looking at a "going concern."

The value of the business may be based on its adjusted earnings times a multiplier for what the business sells for in the industry.

Net income should be adjusted for unusual nonrecurring revenue and expense items. In adjusting net income of the business, we should add back the portion of the following items if personal rather than business related: auto expense, travel expense, and promotion and entertainment expense. Interest expense should also be added back to net income because it is the cost to borrow funds to buy assets or obtain working capital, and as such, is not relevant in determining the operating profit of the business. In the event lease payments arise from a low-cost lease, earnings should be adjusted to arrive at a fair rental charge. Extraordinary items (e.g. Gain on the sale of land) should be removed from earnings to obtain typical earnings. If business assets are being depreciated at an accelerated rate, you should adjust net income upward.

Therefore, the difference between the straight-line method and an accelerated depreciation method should be added back.

We should add back expenses for a closely held business solely for fringe benefits, health plan, pension plan, and life insurance. In addition, we should add back excessive salary representing the difference between the owner's salary and what a reasonable salary would be if we hired someone to do the job. All compensation should be considered including perks. Thus, if the owner gets a salary of $300,000 and a competent worker would get $80,000, the add-back to net income is $220,000.

A tax provision (if none exists) should be made in arriving at the adjusted net income. The tax provision should be based on the current rates for each of the years.

If the company has a significant amount of investment income (e.g. dividend income, interest income, rental income from non-operating property), net income may be reduced for the investment income with taxes being adjusted accordingly. We are primarily concerned with the income from operations.

The adjusted (restated) earnings results in a quality of earning figure. The restated earnings is then multiplied by a multiplier to determine the value of a business. The multiplier should be higher for a low risk business but generally not more than 10. The multiplier should be lower for a high-risk business, often only 1 or 2. Of course, an average multiplier, such as 5, would be used when average risk exists. The P/E ratio for a comparable company would be a good benchmark.

Some investment bankers use in valuation a multiple of the latest year's earnings, or the annual rate of earnings of a current interim period (if representative). An example follows based on a multiplier of one-year profits.

Example 8

Adjusted Net Income for the Current Year	$400,000*
X multiplier	x 4*
Valuation	$1,600,000
*The adjusted net income is computed below:	
Reported Net Income	$325,000
Adjustments:	
Personal expenses (e.g., promotion and entertainment)	50,000
Extraordinary or nonrecurring gain	-60,000
Owner's fringe benefits (e.g., pension plan)	40,000
Excessive owner's salary relative to a reasonable salary	30,000
Interest expense	20,000
Dividend revenue	-10,000
Low-cost rental payments relative to a fair rental charge	-5,000
Excess depreciation from using an accelerated method	10,000
Restated Net Income	$400,000

Typically, a five-year average adjusted historical earnings figure is used. The five years' earnings up to the valuation date demonstrate past earning power. Note that for SEC registration and reporting purposes a five-year period is used. Assuming a simple average is used, the computation follows:

Simple Average Adjusted Earnings over 5 years x Multiplier
(Capitalization Factor, P/E Ratio) of 5 (based on industry standard)
Value of Business

Example 9

Assume the following net incomes:

2x12	$120,000
2x11	$100,000
2x10	$110,000
2x09	$90,000
2x08	$115,000

The multiplier is 4.

Simple Average Earnings = $\dfrac{\$120,000 + \$100,000 + \$110,000 + \$90,000 + \$115,000}{5}$

$$= \frac{\$535,000}{5} \qquad = \$107,000$$

Simple Average Adjusted Earnings over 5 years	$107,000
X Multiplier	x 4
Value of Business	$428,000

Instead of a simple average, a weighted-average adjusted historical earnings figure is recommended. This gives more weight to the most recent years which reflects higher current prices and recent business performance. If a five-year weighted average is used the current year is given a weight of 5 while the first year is assigned a weight of 1. The multiplier is then applied to the weighted-average five-year adjusted earnings to get the value of the business.

Example 10

Year	Net Income	X	Weight	=	Total
2x12	$120,000	X	5	=	$600,000
2x11	$100,000	X	4	=	400,000
2x10	$110,000	X	3	=	330,000
2x09	$90,000	X	2	=	180,000
2x08	$115,000	X	1	=	115,000
			15		$1,625,000

Weighted-average five-year earnings:
$1,625,000/15 = $108,333

Weighted-Average 5-year earnings	$108,333
X Capitalization Factor	x 4*
Capitalization-of-Earnings Valuation	$433,332

If the company's financial statements are not audited, you should insist on an audit to assure accurate reporting.

Has the owner of a closely held company failed to record cash sales to hide income? One way of determining this is to take purchases and add a typical profit markup in the industry. To verify reported profit, you can multiply the sales by the profit margin in the industry. If reported earnings are significantly below what the earnings should be based on the industry standard, there may be some hidden income.

Capitalization of Excess Earnings

The best method is to capitalize excess earnings. The normal rate of return on the weighted-average net tangible assets is subtracted from the weighted-average adjusted earnings to determine excess earnings. It is suggested that the weighting be based on a five-year period. The excess earnings are then capitalized to determine the value of the intangibles (primarily goodwill). The addition of the value of the intangibles and the fair market value of the net tangible assets equals the total valuation. As per IRS Revenue Ruling 68-609, 1968-2 C.B. 327, the IRS recommends this method to value a business for tax purposes. The Revenue Ruling states that the return on average net tangible assets should be the percentage prevailing in the industry. If an industry percentage is not available, an 8% to 10% rate may be used. An 8% return rate is used for a business with a small risk factor and stable earnings while a 10% rate of return is used for a business having a high risk factor and unstable earnings. The capitalization rate for excess earnings should be 15% (multiple of 6.67) for a business with a small risk factor and stable earnings and a 20% capitalization rate (multiple of 5) should be used for a business having a high risk factor and unstable earnings. Thus, the suggested return rate is between 8% to 10%. The range for the capitalization rate may be between 15% to 20%.

Example 11

Weighted-average net tangible assets are computed below:

Year	Amount	X	Weight	=	Total
2x12	$950,000	X	1	=	950,000
2x11	1,000,000	X	2	=	2,000,000
2x10	1,200,000	X	3	=	3,600,000
2x09	1,400,000	X	4	=	5,600,000
2x08	1,500,000	X	5	=	7,500,000
			15		19,650,000

Weighted-Average Net Tangible Assets:

$19,650,000/15 = $1,310,000

Weighted-Average Adjusted Net Income (5 years)—assumed	$600,000

Reasonable Rate of Return on Weighted-Average	
Tangible Net Assets ($1,310,000 x 10%)	131,000
Excess Earnings	469,000
Capitalization Rate (20%)	x 5
Value of Intangibles	$2,345,000
Fair Market Value of Net Tangible Assets	$3,000,000
Capitalization-of-Excess-Earnings Valuation	$5,345,000

Capitalization of Cash Flow

The adjusted cash earnings may be capitalized in arriving at a value for the firm. This method may be suitable for a service business.

Example 12

Adjusted Cash Earnings	$100,000
X Capitalization Factor (25%)	x 4
Capitalization of Cash Flow	$400,000
Less Liabilities Assumes	50,000
Capitalization-of-Cash-Flow Earnings	$350,000

Present Value (Discounting) of Future Cash Flows

A business is worth the discounted value of future cash earnings plus the discounted value of the expected selling price. Cash flow may be a more valid criterion of value than book profits because cash flow can be used for reinvestment. The growth rate in earnings may be based on past growth, future expectations, and the inflation rate. This approach is suggested in a third-party sale situation. We also have more confidence in it when the company is strong in the industry and has solid earnings growth. The problem with the method is the many estimates required of future events. It probably should not be used when there has been an inconsistent trend in earnings.

Step 1: Present Value of Cash Earnings. The earnings should be estimated over future years using an estimated growth rate. A common time frame for a cash flow valuation is 10 years. Once the future earnings are determined, they should be discounted. Future earnings may be based on the prior years' earnings and the current profit margin applied to sales. Cash earnings equals net income plus noncash expense adjustments such as depreciation.

Step 2: Present Value of Sales Price. The present value of the expected selling price of the business at the date of sale should be determined. This residual value may be based on a multiple of earnings or cash flow, expected market value, and so on.

You may use as the discount rate the minimum acceptable return to the buyer for investing in the target company. The discount rate may take into account the usual return rate for money, inflation rate, a risk premium (based on such factors as local market conditions, earnings instability, and level of debt), and maybe a premium for the illiquidity of the investment. If the risk-free interest rate is 7% (on government bonds), the risk premium is 8%, and the illiquidity premium is 7%, the capitalization (discount) will be 22%. The risk premium may range from 5% to 10%, while the illiquidity premium may range from 5% to 15%. Some evaluators simply use as the discount rate the market interest rate of a low-risk asset investment. *Note:* If the net incremental cash flows to the acquiring firm's shareholders are to be valued, the discount rate used should be the cost of equity capital. Moreover, this rate should reflect the risk associated with the use of funds rather than their source. The rate therefore should not be the cost of capital of the acquiring firm but rather the cost of equity of the combined firm after the combination.

Assuming you expect to hold the business for 14 years, and anticipate a 12% rate of return and constant earnings each year, the value of the business is based on:

For cash earnings: Present value of an annuity for $n = 14$, $i = 12\%$ (Table 2 in the Appendix)

For selling price: Present value of $1 for $n = 14$, $i = 12\%$ (Table 1 in the Appendix)

Total Present Value

If earnings grow at an 8% rate, a Present Value of $1 table would be used to discount the annual earnings, which would change each year.

Example 13

In 2x13, the net income is $220,000. Earnings are expected to grow at 8% per year. The discount rate is 10%. You estimate that the business is worth the discounted value of future earnings.

The valuation equals:

Net Income Year (based on an 8% growth rate)		PV of $1 Factor (at 10% interest) (Table 1)	Present Value
2x13	$200,000 x	0.909	$181,800
2x14	208,000 x	0.826	171,808
2x15	224,600 x	0.751	168,675
2x16	242,568 x	0.683	165,674
2x17	261,973 x	0.621	162,685
Present Value of Future Earnings			$850,642

If the expected selling price at the end of year 2x17 is $600,000, the valuation of the business equals:

Present value of earnings	$850,642
Selling price in 2x17 $600,000 x .621	372,600
Valuation	$1,223,242

Example 14 (A Comprehensive Case)

ACQ's Home Repair Company, a regional hardware chain that specializes in "do-it-yourself" materials and equipment rentals, is cash rich because of several consecutive good years. One of the alternative uses for the excess funds is an acquisition. Julie Kerr, ACQ's CFO, has been asked to place a value on a potential target, TGT's Hardware, a small chain that operates in an adjacent state, and she has enlisted your help. The table below indicates Kerr's estimates of TGT's earnings potential if it came under ACQ's management.

(In millions of dollars).

	2012	2013	2014	2015
Net sales	$60.0	$90.0	$112.5	$127.5
Cost of goods sold (60%)	$36.0	$54.0	$67.5	$76.5
Selling/Administrative expense	$4.5	$6.0	$7.5	$9.0
Interest expense	$3.0	$4.5	$4.5	$6.0
Necessary retained earnings	$0.0	$7.5	$6.0	$4.5

The interest expense listed here includes the interest (1) on TGT's existing debt, (2) on new debt that ACQ's would issue to help finance the acquisition, and (3) on new debt

49

expected to be issued over time to help finance expansion within the new "H Division," the code name given to the target firm. The retentions represent earnings that will be reinvested within the H Division to help finance its growth.

TGT's Hardware currently uses 40 percent debt financing, and it pays federal-plus-state taxes at a 30 percent rate. Security analysts estimate TGT's beta to be 1.2. If the acquisition were to take place, ACQ's would increase TGT's debt ratio to 50 percent, which would increase its beta to 1.3. Further, because ACQ's is highly profitable, taxes on the consolidated firm would be 40 percent. Kerr realizes that TGT's Hardware also generates depreciation cash flows, but she believes that these funds would have to be reinvested within the division to replace worn-out equipment.

Kerr estimates the risk-free rate to be 9 percent and the market risk premium to be 4 percent. She also estimates that net cash flows after 2015 will grow at a constant rate of 6 percent. The following is the H Division's cash flow statements for 2012 through 2015, assuming the acquisition is made.

	(In millions of dollars)			
	2012	**2013**	**2014**	**2015**
Net sales	$60.0	$90.0	$112.5	$127.5
Cost of goods sold (60%)	$36.0	$54.0	$67.5	$76.5
Selling/Administrative expense	$4.5	$6.0	$7.5	$9.0
Interest expense(a)	$3.0	$4.5	$4.5	$6.0
EBT	$16.5	$25.5	$33.0	$36.0
Taxes (40%) (b)	$6.6	$10.2	$13.2	$14.4
Net Income	$9.9	$15.3	$19.8	$21.6
Less: retentions needed for growth (c)	$0.0	$7.5	$6.0	$4.5
Cash Flow	$9.9	$7.8	$13.8	$17.1
Plus: terminal value (d)	——	——	——	$566.4
Net Cash Flow to ACQ (e)	$9.9	$7.8	$13.8	$583.5
NPV = $436.58				

Note:
  (a) Interest payments are estimates based on TGT's existing debt, plus additional debt required to finance growth.
  (b) ACQ will file a consolidated tax return after the merger. Thus, the taxes shown here are the full corporate taxes attributable to TGT's operations: there will be no additional taxes on any cash flows passed from TGT to ACQ.
  (c) Some of the cash flows generated by the TGT subsidiary after the merger must be retained to finance asset replacements and growth, while some will be transferred to ACQ to pay dividends on its stock or for redeployment

within the corporation. These retentions are net of any additional debt used to help finance growth.

(d) TGT's available cash flows are expected to grow at a constant 6 percent rate after 2015. The value of all post-2015 cash flows as of December 31, 2015, is estimated by use of the constant growth model to be $566.44 million:

$$P_o = \frac{CF_{2016}}{R\text{-}g} = \frac{(\$21.6 - \$4.5)(1.06)}{0.092 - 0.06} = \$566.44 \text{ million}$$

Where r = required rate of return.

Note: T estimated 9.2 percent cost of equity is computed, using the CAPM model.

Required rate of return = risk-free rate + beta x market risk premium = 4% + 1.3 (4%) = 9.2%

(e) These are the net cash flows projected to be available to ACQ by virtue of the acquisition. The cash flows could be used for dividend payments to ACQ's stockholders, to finance asset expansion in ACQ's other divisions and subsidiaries, and so on.

(f) The $436.58 million is the PV at the end of 2015 of the stream of cash flows for Year 2016 and thereafter.

Note that these statements are identical to standard capital budgeting cash flow statements except that both interest expense and retentions are included in merger analysis. In straight capital budgeting, all debt involved is new debt that is issued to fund the asset additions. Hence, the debt involved all costs the same and this cost is accounted for by discounting the cash flows at the firm's cost of capital. However, in a merger the acquiring firm usually both assumes the existing debt of the target and issues new debt to help finance the takeover. Thus, the debt involved has different costs, and hence cannot be accounted for as a single cost in the cost of capital. The easiest solution is to explicitly include interest expense in the cash flow statement.

With respect to retentions, all of the cash flows from an individual project are available for use throughout the firm, but some of the cash flows generated by an acquisition are generally retained with the new division to help finance its growth. Since such retentions are not available to the parent company for use elsewhere, they must be deducted in the cash flow statement.

With interest expense and retentions included in the cash flow statements, the cash flows are residuals that are available to the acquiring firm's equity holders. ACQ's management could pay these out as dividends or reinvest them in other divisions of the firm, as they see fit.   *Note*: If another firm were valuing TGT's, they would probably obtain an estimate different from $436.58 million. Most important, the synergies involved would likely be different, and hence the cash flow estimates would differ. Also, another potential acquirer might use different financing, or have a different tax rate, and hence estimate a different discount rate.

Example 15

Assume in Example 14 that TGT's has 10 million shares outstanding. These shares are traded relatively infrequently, but the last trade, made several weeks ago, was at a price of $35 per share. Should ACQ's make an offer for TGT's? If so, how much should it offer per share? With a current price of $35 per share and 10 million shares outstanding, TGT's current market value is $35(10) = $350 million. Since TGT's expected value to ACQ's is $436.58 million, it appears that the merger would be beneficial to both sets of stockholders. The difference, $436.58 - $350 = $86.58 million, is the added value to be apportioned between the stockholders of both firms. The offering range is from $9 per share to $436.58/10 = $43.66 per share. At $35, all of the benefit of the merger goes to ACQ's shareholders, while at $43.66, all of the value created goes to TGT's shareholders. If ACQ's offers more than $43.66 per share, then wealth would be transferred from ACQ's stockholders to TGT's stockholders.

As to the actual offering price, ACQ's should make the offer as low as possible, yet acceptable to TGT's shareholders. A low initial offer, say $35.50 per share, would probably be rejected and the effort wasted. Further, the offer may influence other potential suitors to consider TGT's, and they could end up outbidding ACQ's. Conversely, a high price, say $44, passes almost all of the gain to TGT's stockholders, and ACQ's managers should retain as much of the synergistic value as possible for their own shareholders.

Operating Cash Flow

Some businesses may be valued at a multiple of operating cash flow. For example, radio and TV stations often sell for between 8 to 12 times operating cash flow.

Book Value (Net Worth)

The business may be valued based on the book value of the net assets (assets less liabilities) at the most recent balance sheet date. This method is unrealistic because it does not take into account current values. It may be appropriate only when it is impossible to determine fair value of net assets and/or goodwill. However, book value may be adjusted for obvious understatements such as excess depreciation, LIFO reserve, favorable leases, and for low debt (e.g., low rental payments or unfounded pension and postretirement benefits). Unfortunately, it may be difficult for a buying company to have access to information regarding these adjustments.

Tangible Net Worth

The valuation of the company is its tangible net worth for the current year equal to:
Stockholders' Equity
Less: Intangible Assets
Tangible Net Worth

Economic Net Worth (Adjusted Book Value)

Economic net worth equals:
Fair Market Value of Net Assets
Plus: Goodwill (as per agreement)
Economic Net Worth
Fair Market Value of Net Assets

The fair market value of the net tangible assets of the business may be determined through independent appraisal. To it, we add the value of the goodwill (if any). Note that goodwill applies to such aspects as reputation of the company, customer base, and high quality merchandise. IRS Appeals and Review Memorandums (ARM) 34 and 38 present formula methods to value goodwill. In the case of a small business, a business broker may be retained to do the appraisal of property, plant, and equipment. A business broker is experienced because he or she puts together the purchase of small businesses. According to Equitable Business Brokers, about 25% of businesses changing hands are sold through business brokers. Typically the fair value of the net tangible assets (assets less liabilities) is higher than book value.

The general practice is to value inventory at a maximum value of cost. IRS Revenue Procedure 77-12 provides acceptable ways to allocate a lump-sum purchase price to inventories.

Unrecognized and unrecorded liabilities should be considered when determining the fair market value of net assets. For example, one company the author consulted had both an unrecorded liability for liquidated damages for nonunion contracts of $3,100,000 and an unrecorded liability for $4,900,000 related to the estimated employer final withdrawal liability. Obviously, as a result of unrecorded liabilities the value of a business will be reduced further.

A tax liability may also exist that has not been recognized in the accounts. For example, the company's tax position may be adjusted by the IRS which is currently auditing the tax return. This contingent liability should be considered in valuing the business.

In a similar vein, unrecorded and undervalued assets, such as customer lists, patents, and licensing agreements, should be considered because they increase the value of the business.

Note: IRS Revenue Ruling 35-193 approves only those approaches where valuations can be determined separately for tangible and intangible assets.

Liquidation Value

Liquidation value is a conservative figure of value because it does not take into account the earning power of the business. Liquidation value is a "floor" price in negotiations. Liquidation value is the estimated value of the company's assets, assuming their conversion into cash in a short time period. All liabilities and the costs of liquidating the business (e.g. appraisal fees, real estate fees, legal and accounting fees, recapture taxes) are subtracted from the total cash to obtain net liquidation value.

Liquidation value may be computed based on an orderly liquidation or a forced (rapid) liquidation. In the case of the latter, there will obviously be a lower value.

Replacement Cost

Replacement cost ("new") is the cost of duplicating from scratch the business' assets on an "as-if -new" basis. It will typically result in a higher figure than book value or fair market value of existing assets. Replacement cost provides a meaningful basis of comparison with other methods but should not be used as the acquisition value. A more accurate indicator of value is when replacement cost is adjusted for relevant depreciation and obsolescence.

Secured-Loan Value

The secured-loan value reflects the borrowing power of the seller's assets. Typically, banks will lend up to 90% of accounts receivable and 10%-60% of the value of inventory depending on how much represents finished goods, work-in-process, and raw materials. The least percentage amount will be work-in-process, and raw materials. The least percentage amount will be work-in-process because of its greater realization risk and difficulty of sale. Also considered are turnover rates.

Gross Revenue Multiplier

The value of the business may be determined by multiplying the revenue by the gross revenue multiplier common in the industry. This approach may be used when earnings are questionable.

Example 16

If revenue is $14,000,000 and the multiplier is .2, the valuation is: $14,000,000 x .2 = $2,800,000.

In a similar fashion, insurance agencies often sell for about 150% of annual commissions.

Profit Margin/Capitalization Rate

The profit margin divided by the capitalization rate provides a multiplier which is then applied to revenue. A multiplier of revenue that a company would sell at is the company's profit margin. The profit margin may be based on the industry's average. The formula is:

$$\frac{\text{Profit Margin}}{\text{Capitalization Rate}} = \text{Multiplier}$$

The capitalization rate in earnings is the return demanded by investors. In arriving at a capitalization rate, the prime interest rate may be taken into account. The multiplier is what the buyer is willing to pay.

Example 17

Assume sales of $14,000,000, a profit margin of 5%, and a capitalization rate of 20%. The multiplier is 25% (5%/20%). The valuation is:

Sales x 25%

$14,000,000 x 25% = $3,500,000

The IRS and the courts have considered recent sales as an important factor.

Price-Earnings Factor

The value of a business may be based on the price-earnings factor applied to current (or expected) earnings per share (EPS). For publicly traded companies, the P/E ratio is known.

Valuation for a privately held company is more difficult. Historical earnings must be adjusted for a closely held company to be consistent with the reported earnings of a public company. After suitable adjustments have been made, the average P/E ratio for the industry or for several comparable public companies is used to arrive at a value. Typically, a premium is added to the value estimate to incorporate uncertainty and additional risk and lack of marketability associated with private companies. A variation of the P/E method may also be used. Assuming an expected earnings growth rate of the seller and a desired ROI, the acquirer determines an earnings multiple he or she pays to achieve the ROI goal. Under this approach, the buyer determines the price he or she would be willing to pay instead of using a stock-market-related price.

Example 18

Net income	$800,000
Outstanding shares	100,000
EPS	$8
P/E Multiple	x10
Market Price per Share	$80
X Number of Shares Outstanding	x 100,000
Price-Earnings Valuation	$8,000,000

Comparative Values of Similar Going Concerns

What would someone pay for this business? Reference may be made to the market price of similar publicly traded companies. Under this approach, you obtain the market prices of companies in the industry similar in nature to the one being examined. Recent sales prices of similar businesses may be used and an average taken. Upward or downward adjustments to this average will be made depending on the particular circumstances of the company being valued.

There are two ways of arriving at an adjusted average value for a company based on comparable transactions. Under the equivalency adjustment method, you make an adjustment to each transaction before averaging based on such factors as size, profitability, earnings stability and transaction structure. Transactions are adjusted downward if it appears that a higher price was paid than would be appropriate for the target company, and vice versa. The average of the adjusted comparables approximates the estimated value of the target company. With the simple averaging method, you determine a simple average of the comparable transaction after excluding noncomparable cases and adjust the target company's price insofar as it differs from the average features of the company's purchases in comparable transactions. The former approach is suggested where extensive data are available on the comparable transactions and where they differ substantially in their features. The latter approach is preferable where the comparable transactions are broadly similar or where many comparable transactions have occurred.

While a perfect match is not possible, the companies should be reasonably similar (e.g. size, product, structure, geographic location, diversity). The comparable transactions value will often be higher than the market value of the target's stock price. Several sources of industry information are Standard & Poor's Dow Jones-Irwin, on-line information services, and trade association's reports. Extensive databases exist to assist in the analysis of merger-market history.

Example 19

A competing company has just been sold for $6,000,000. We believe the company is worth 90% of the competing business. Therefore, the valuation is $5,400,000.

Sales of Stock

The value of the business may be based on the outstanding shares times the market price of the stock. For an actively traded stock, the stock price provides an important benchmark. For a thinly traded stock, the stock price may not reflect an informed market consensus. Typically, the market price of the stock should be based on a discounted amount from the current market price since if all the shares are being sold, the market price per share may drop somewhat based on the demand-supply relationship. Further, market value of stock is of use only in planning the actual strategy of acquiring a target company since the stock may be overvalued or undervalued relative to the worth of the target company to the acquirer.

Combination of Methods

The value of the business may be approximated by determining the average value of two or more methods.

Example 20

Assume that the fair market value of net assets approach gives a value of $2,100,000, while the capitalization of excess earnings method provides a value of $2,500,000. The value of the business would then be the average of these two methods, or $2,300,000 ($2,100,000 + $2,500,00)/2.

Some courts have found a combination of methods supportable as long as greater weight is given to the earning methods. S. Pratt writes that the most weight should be placed on the earning approaches and less on the asset approaches.

Example 21

Using the same information as in the prior example, if a 2 weight were assigned to the earnings approach and a 1 weight were assigned to the fair market value of net assets method, the valuation would be:

Method	Amount	x	Weight	=	Total
Fair Market Value of Net Assets	$2,100,000	x	1		$2,100,000
Capitalization-of-Excess Earnings	2,500,000	x	2		5,000,000
			3		$7,100,000
					/3
Valuation					$2,366,667

Accounting Adjustments

Material accounting adjustments should be made to the acquired company's figures to place them on a comparable basis to those of the acquirer. Adjustments should be made, where practical, for savings in administrative, technical, sales, plant, and clerical personnel costs resulting from the combination. These savings arise from the elimination of duplicate personnel, plant, office, and warehouse facilities. Savings in freight may result from the combination by shifting production to plants closer to markets.

Q ratio

A firm's Q ratio equals the market value of the firm's securities ÷ replacement cost of its assets. A ratio greater than one means that a firm is earning returns greater than the amount invested. For this reason, a company with a ratio exceeding one should attract new resources and competition. It is also called *Tobin's Q*. The higher the Q-ratio, the greater the competitive advantage. The notion of this ratio holds that a firm's market value ultimately equals the replacement cost of its tangible assets. Another aspect of undervaluation is that a firm's Q ratio may be less than one.

Summary

The price to be paid for a business depends upon many factors including the seller's strengths, weaknesses and prospects. The buyer's objectives and requirements are also relevant. A total cash transaction justifies a lower price than an installment sale because with an installment sale there are the uncertainties of cash collection and the time value of money.

When valuing a company, more weight should be placed on the earnings approaches and less on the asset approaches. Valuation may be based on a combined approach of methods including earnings and asset valuation. In deriving a value, industry standards may be quite helpful. Consideration should be given to adjusted cash earnings, gross revenue, fair value of net assets, and recent sales of similar businesses. A proper valuation is needed so as to come up with a realistic price that is fair to all concerned parties. IRS Revenue Procedure 66-49 discusses how the IRS comes up with its valuations. Some of the contents of what should be in a valuation report are mentioned.

Accounting, Reporting and Disclosures for Business Combinations

Business combinations in the form of mergers and acquisitions occur when companies choose to combine (rather than grow internally) to take advantage of cost efficiencies or transform their businesses to the next level. The result of a business combination is that the combined company may have additional product offerings, greater geographic presence, increased market share, as well as control over all sources of production and product distribution (vertical integration). The accountant is frequently called upon to advise management of the impact of proposed combinations, as well as to prepare consolidated financial statements for completed transactions. Knowledge of the emerging accounting rules in this area is critical in supporting both functions.

With the exception of the elimination of pooling of interests for new acquisitions (in 2001) and the required consolidation of variable interest entities (revised in 2003), the accounting rules for business combinations and consolidations remained largely unchanged for over 50 years until December 2007, when the FASB, after many years of deliberation, simultaneously issued two new standards, FASB Statement No. 141R (FASB-141R), *Business Combinations* (ASC 805) (a revision of FASB Statement No. 141), and FASB Statement No.160 (FASB-160), *Noncontrolling Interests in Consolidated Financial Statements*—An Amendment of ARB No. 51 (ASC 810-10-65-1). These statements, which require prospective treatment for new business combinations having fiscal years beginning after December 15, 2008, mandate what is referred to as the acquisition method. Moreover, the purchase method of accounting will no longer be permitted for acquisitions closed after the effective date of the new rules. *Note:* ASC 805 (FSA-141R) completes a joint effort by the FASB and IASB to standardize the reporting for business combinations as part of the international convergence project. IASB's IFRS 3, *Business Combinations* was issued in 2007 and for the most part, mirrors the rules found in the newly issued ASC 805 (FSA-141R).

A critical distinction is that the new rules abandon the historical cost-based structure of accounting for acquisitions at the price paid and require that consolidation of the acquiree is at "business fair value." As retroactive adoption of the new standards is not permitted, mergers completed before the effective date must continue to be treated in accordance with the accounting standards that were in effect at the date of the original business combination. Therefore, there will continue to be many mergers that will be "grandfathered" under the accounting rules in existence at the dates they were completed (i.e., purchase method and pooling of interests method).

Contrast of Acquisition Method with Purchase and Pooling of Interest Methods

Prior to the effective dates of ASC 805 (FSA-141R).and ASC 810, Consolidation (FAS-160)., previously completed business combinations were accounted for under the purchase method or the pooling of interest method. Since the new rules are grandfathered, those business combinations will continue to be accounted for under the rules that were in place at the time the transaction closed.

A listing of the main points of each method is as follows:

A. Acquisition method (effective for new acquisitions by acquirers having fiscal years beginning after December 15, 2008):
   - Focus is on fair value of the acquired entity.
   - Direct combination costs are expensed.
   - Stock issuance costs are treated as a reduction of Additional Paid in Capital.
   - Bargain purchase is treated as income to the acquirer.
   - Fair value of contingent consideration at acquisition date is considered part of the fair value of the acquired entity.
   - Subsequent resolution of contingent consideration at a value different from that recorded at acquisition date is run through the income statement.
   - Acquiree in process research and development costs and other purchased intangibles are recorded at fair value at acquisition date.
   - Preacquisition contingencies that are resolved after the acquisition closing date are expensed.
   - Acquiree assets and liabilities are reported in the consolidated entity at fair value.

B. Purchase method (effective for acquisitions closed prior to December 15, 2008, that have been accounted for under the purchase method):
   - Acquisitions continue to be accounted for under the purchase method.
   - Focus is on historical cost of the acquisition (i.e., the price paid to acquire an entity).
   - Direct combination costs are capitalized as part of the investment cost.
   - Stock issuance costs are treated as a reduction of Additional Paid in Capital.
   - Bargain purchase results in a proportional reduction of noncurrent assets of the acquiree with any excess treated as an extraordinary gain.
   - Contingent consideration is not recorded as part of acquisition cost until it is subsequently resolved. (Note: If the resolution of the contingency

requires an additional payment to be made by the acquirer, that payment will either increase goodwill or lessen the reduction to noncurrent assets in the case of a bargain purchase).

▷ Acquiree in process research and development costs is included in acquisition cost only where considered either technologically feasible or subject to alternative future use.

▷ Assets and liabilities of the acquiree are reported at fair value, subject to any reduction in acquiree noncurrent assets due to a bargain purchase.

C. Pooling of Interest method (effective for acquisitions completed prior to June 30, 2001, assuming they met all 12 of the specific criteria in existence at that time):

▷ Acquisitions will continue to be consolidated under this method, until the entities are sold, closed, or otherwise disposed of.

▷ Assets and liabilities are consolidated at their book values.

▷ There are no adjustments to either the balance sheet (fair value allocations) or the income statement (amortization of fair value adjustments).

▷ Income and expense of the acquiree are reported retrospectively; that is, they are retroactively restated for all periods presented.

The following table presents the main differences between the acquisition and purchase methods of accounting:

Acquisition Method vs. Purchase Method

	New Rules (Acquisition Method) ASC 805 (FAS-141R); ASC 810 (FAS-160)	Old Rules (Purchase Method) ASC 805 (FAS-141); ASC 810 (ARB 51)
Focus	Fair value of entity acquired, referred to as "business fair value"	Historical cost; i.e., price paid to acquire the entity
Direct combination costs	Expensed	Treated as part of cost of acquisition
Bargain purchase	Recognize as income on transaction closing date	Reduce noncurrent assets proportionately; any excess is extraordinary gain
Stock issuance costs	Decrease (debit) to Additional Paid In Capital	Same

	New Rules (Acquisition Method) ASC 805 (FAS-141R); ASC 810 (FAS-160)	Old Rules (Purchase Method) ASC 805 (FAS-141); ASC 810 (ARB 51)
Contingent consideration	Recorded at fair value at transaction closing date; subsequent changes in fair value recorded in income statement	Not recorded as part of acquisition cost until contingency is resolved. This will result in additional goodwill or less reduction to noncurrent assets (bargain purchase)
In process research and development costs	Capitalize at fair value as intangible assets, subject to impairment testing or amortization	Expensed
Preacquisition contingencies	Contractual contingencies recorded at fair value; noncontractual contingencies recorded at fair value if they meet "more likely than not" criteria for definition of an asset or liability	Not recorded unless FAS-5 criteria are met (i.e., probable and reasonably estimable
Valuation of equity issued	Fair value at transaction closing date	Fair value at the date the acquisition is announced
Other intangible assets	Recorded at fair value	Recorded as part of investment cost if meeting contractual criteria (e.g., patents) or separability (e.g., technology)

Steps to Accounting under the Acquisition Method

The following steps are taken in accounting for a business combination under the acquisition method:

1. Assets and liabilities of the acquired business are recorded at fair market value as follows: Trading securities are at market value. Receivables are recorded at the discounted present value of amounts to be received using current interest rates, less allowance for bad debts and collection costs. Raw materials are recorded at current replacement cost. Work in process is recorded at estimated net realizable value of finished goods less the costs to complete and the profit allowance. Finished goods are recorded

at estimated net realizable value less a reasonable profit allowance (lower limit). Fixed assets to be used in the business are recorded at replacement cost. If the fixed assets are to be sold, they are recorded at fair value less cost to sell. Intangibles and other assets are recognized at appraised values. Any duplicate assets that are to be disposed of are recorded at estimated net salvage value. If there is no net salvage value, a zero valuation is assigned. Liabilities are typically recorded at the discounted present value of amounts to be paid based on current interest rates.

2. The excess of the fair value of consideration transferred over the fair value of net assets acquired is assigned to goodwill, which is subject to an annual impairment test.

3. Goodwill previously recorded by the acquiree is not brought forward.

4. The excess of the fair value of net assets received over the fair value of consideration transferred is recorded as a gain on bargain purchases.

5. None of the stockholders' equity accounts of the acquired company is shown on the acquirer's books or in the consolidated financial statements.

6. Net income of the acquired business is recognized from the acquisition date to year-end.

7. Direct costs of the acquisition (e.g., legal, accounting, consulting, engineering evaluation, appraisal, and finders' fees) are expensed. Indirect and general costs (internal costs) are also expensed as incurred. If the acquirer pays fees to an investment banker for advice and assistance, such costs must be expensed. The costs of registering and issuing any debt or equity securities to effect the combination are accounted for as any other issue cost; that is, the issuance cost for debt is deferred and amortized over the term of the debt using the interest method, and the cost of issuing stock (e.g., underwriting fees) is a reduction of additional paid-in-capital. Liabilities and commitments for the costs of closing an acquired company's plant are considered direct costs of the acquisition and are expensed. However, the costs of closing a duplicate plant of the acquirer are not part of the acquisition cost.

According to ASC 805-20-55-51, termination or employee relocation costs arising because of a business combination should be accrued when the combination is consummated.

A purchase of stock appreciation rights (awards) or stock options by an acquired company related to a business combination should be accounted for as compensation expense rather than as an element of acquisition cost by the acquirer.

If debt securities are issued in the acquisition, they should be recorded at their fair value based on the present value of the debt payments discounted at the market interest rate. Any difference between face value and present value is recorded as discount or premium on the debt.

In determining the fair value of securities issued in a business combination, consideration should be given to the quantity issued, price variability, and issue costs.

There is a step-by-step acquisition process to be followed:

▶ If control is not achieved on the initial purchase, the subsidiary is not included in consolidation until control has been achieved.

▶ After the parent owns more than 50% of the subsidiary, a retroactive adjustment is required, including the subsidiary's profits in consolidated retained earnings, in a step-by-step manner starting with the original investment.

▶ The subsidiary's profits are included in ownership years at the applicable percentage owned.

Example 22

On October 31, 2X13, Kravis Company bought for cash at $10 per share all 300,000 of Hartman's outstanding common stock. It is agreed that the purchase price equals business fair value. At October 31, 2X13, Hartman's balance sheet showed a book value of net assets of $2,500,000. At that date, the fair value of Hartman's fixed assets exceeded its book value by $300,000. In the October 31, 2X13 consolidated balance sheet, Kravis reports goodwill of $200,000, computed as follows:

Fair value of consideration transferred ($10@300,000 shares)	$3,000,000
Book value of net assets acquired	2,500,000
Excess of cost over book value	$ 500,000
Excess of fair value over book value of fixed assets	300,000
Goodwill	$ 200,000

Example 23

ABC Co. purchases 100% interest in common stock of DEF Co. for $1,800,000.

The journal entry to reflect the initial investment is:

Investment in DEF Company	1,800,000	
Cash		1,800,000

Example 24

Moses Company bought 100% of Rolo Company in a business combination on September 30, 2X13. During 2X13, Moses declared dividends of $20,000 per quarter, and Rolo declared quarterly dividends of $5,000. The dividends declared to be reported in December 31, 20X8, consolidated retained earnings under the acquisition method are $80,000 (those paid by Moses only). The dividends paid by Rolo go to Moses and are eliminated in consolidation.

Example 25

On June 30, 2X13, Harris Company exchanged 300,000 shares of its $10 par value common stock for all of Blake Company's common stock. The fair market value of Harris Company's common stock issued equals the carrying value of Blake's net assets. Both entities will continue their separate businesses and operations. The following data are presented:

	Harris	Blake
Retained earnings—12/31/2X12	$3,000,000	$900,000
Dividends paid—4/1/2X13	700,000	
Net income—1/1/2X13 to 6/30/2X13	850,000	250,000

If the acquisition method was used, the balance in retained earnings to be presented by the Harris Company in its June 30, 20X13, consolidated balance sheet would be based on the parent's retained earnings as follows:

Balance, 12/31/2X12	$3,000,000
Net income—1/1/2X13-6/30/2X13	850,000
Dividends paid—4/1/2X13	(700,000)
Retained earnings—6/30/2X13	$3,150,000

Earnings of Blake Company prior to the acquisition date are not included in consolidated retained earnings.

If there is an exchange by a partly owned subsidiary of its common stock for the voting common stock of the parent company, this *downstream merger* transaction is treated as a purchase.

Example 26

Business Combination Accounted for under the Acquisition Method

ABC Company issues 50,000 shares on December 1, 2X12, to acquire all of XYZ Company's outstanding shares. This transaction will be accounted for under the acquisition method, with XYZ Company becoming a 100%-owned subsidiary of ABC Company.

ABC Company

Shares issued to acquire XYZ Company:	50,000
Par value:	$ 3
Fair value:	$ 10

XYZ Company

Total shares outstanding:	10,000
Par value:	$ 10

Out-of-Pocket Costs of Business Combination

Legal fees related to business combination:	$35,000
SEC stock registration related costs:	$15,000
Total:	$50,000

ABC Company and XYZ Company Separate Balance Sheets (prior to combination) As of Dec. 31, 2X12

	ABC Company	XYZ Company
ASSETS		
Current assets	900,000	135,000
Property, plant, and equipment (net)	2,500,000	400,000
Other assets	-	35,000
Total Assets	3,400,000	570,000
LIABILITIES & EQUITY		
Current liabilities	500,000	120,000
Long-term liabilities	1,200,000	200,000
Common stock, ABC Company	900,000	
Common stock, XYZ Company		100,000
Paid-in-capital	300,000	50,000
Retained earnings	500,000	100,000
Total liabilities and equity	3,400,000	570,000

It is assumed that there were no intercompany transactions prior to the business combination. Moreover, there were no contingent considerations related to this combination. The effect of income taxes is disregarded in this example.

ABC will record its investment in XYZ as follows:

12/31/2X12	Investment in XYZ Company	500,000	
	Common stock		150,000
	Additional Paid-in-capital		350,000

To record issuance of ABC shares in exchange for all of XYZ shares in a purchase type business combination.

12/31/2X12	Operating expenses	35,000	
	Additional Paid-in-capital	15,000	
	Cash		50,000

To record direct combination costs and stock issuance costs.

The fair value for XYZ Company's assets and liabilities differs from the carrying amount at the date of acquisition as follows:

	Carrying Amount	Fair Value
Inventory (part of current assets)	100,000	125,000
Plant assets	400,000	550,000
Long-term liabilities	200,000	170,000

Thus, XYZ's assets and liabilities in terms of fair values are as follows:

ASSETS

Current assets	160,000*	
Property, plant, and equipment (net)	550,000	
Other assets	35,000	
Total assets		745,000

LIABILITIES

Current liabilities	120,000	
Long-term liabilities	170,000	
Total liabilities		290,000
Fair value of XYZ		455,000

*[135,000+(125,000-100,000)]

The Goodwill generated by the acquisition may be calculated as follows:

ABC's total investment in XYZ	500,000
Less: fair value of XYZ	455,000
Goodwill	45,000

ABC Company and Subsidiary Consolidated Balance Sheet As of Dec. 31, 2X13

	ABC Company	XYZ Company	Eliminations Increases (Decreases)	Consolidated
ASSETS				
Current assets	850,000	135,000	25,000	1,010,000
Investment in XYZ	500,000		(500,000)	-
Property, plant, and equipment (net)	2,500,000	400,000	150,000	3,050,000
Other assets		35,000	-	35,000
Goodwill		45,000	45,000	
Total assets	3,850,000	570,000	(280,000)	4,140,000
LIABILITIES & EQUITY				
Current liabilities	500,000	120,000		620,000
Long-term liabilities	1,200,000	200,000	(30,000)	1,370,000
Common stock, ABC Company	1,050,000			1,050,000
Common stock, XYZ Company		100,000	(100,000)	-
Additional Paid-incapital	635,000	50,000	(50,000)	635,000
Retained earnings	465,000*	100,000	(100,000)	500,000
Total liabilities and equity	3,850,000	570,000	(280,000)	4,140,000

* 500,000-35,000 direct combination costs.

Research and Development Costs Acquired as Part of a Business Combination

ASC 805-20-30 requires that research and development assets acquired in a business combination of a business be initially recognized and measured at fair value, even if those assets do not have alternative future use. Subsequent to initial recording, such research and development costs are subject to the annual impairment review prescribed under ASC 350. The scope of this accounting extends to all acquired or purchased tangible and intangible assets resulting from research and development activities, including patents, blueprints, formulas, and designs for new products and processes. It also includes materials and supplies, and equipment and facilities used by the acquiree in its research and development activities.

Income Taxes

For business combinations occurring after the effective date of this statement, the acquiring company shall recognize a deferred tax asset or liability associated with temporary differences between the assigned value on the books and the tax bases of net assets acquired, in accordance with ASC 805-740-05-1. The acquirer shall also account for potential tax effects of temporary differences, carryforwards, and any income tax uncertainties of the acquiree in accordance with ASC 740-10.

For business transactions occurring before the effective date of the Statement, the acquirer shall not adjust the accounting for prior business combinations for previously recognized changes in acquired tax uncertainties or previously recognized changes in the valuation allowance for acquired deferred tax assets.

Disclosures

For each acquisition that occurs during the reporting period or after the reporting period but before financial statements are issued, the acquirer must disclose:

- ▶ Name and description of the acquiree.
- ▶ Acquisition date.
- ▶ Percentage of voting interest acquired.
- ▶ Rationale for the business combination and how the acquirer obtained control of the acquiree.
- ▶ Qualitative factors supporting any goodwill from the transaction (e.g., expected synergies from combined operations or description of intangible assets not qualifying for separate recognition).
- ▶ Fair value of total consideration transferred, as well as fair value of each component.
- ▶ Amount and description of any contingent consideration, as well as a discussion of the circumstances in which payment will be made; also included should be a range of possible outcomes or, if a range cannot be estimated, the reasons why.
- ▶ Amounts recognized at the acquisition date for each major class of assets acquired and liabilities assumed.
- ▶ Nature of recognized and unrecognized contingencies along with a range of possible outcomes.
- ▶ Total goodwill expected to be deducted for tax purposes.
- ▶ If acquirer is required to disclose segment information, the amount of goodwill by reportable segment (this information will be used in the goodwill impairment test).

▶ Where acquirer and acquiree have previously had a business relationship, any amounts that are not part of the exchange in the business combination between the acquirer and acquiree should be identified.

▶ Any acquisition-related costs and, where reported in the financial statements, that is, expense, reduction of paid in capital, or other category.

▶ For any bargain purchase, the amount of the gain included in the consolidated income statement and the reason why the business combination resulted in a gain.

▶ Fair value of any noncontrolling interest and valuation techniques used to measure fair value.

▶ For step acquisitions, the fair value of any equity interest held immediately prior to the acquisition date and the amount of gain or loss recognized as a result of remeasuring to fair value.

▶ For public companies, the amount of revenue and earnings subsequent to the acquisition date, reported in the consolidated income statement.

As clarified by Accounting Standards Update (ASU) No. 2010-29 in December 2010, supplemental pro forma information, showing revenue and earnings of the acquiree as though the business combination occurred as of the beginning of the comparable annual reporting period. For example, if a calendar year-end company completed a business combination in April 2011, disclosures would be provided as if the business combination occurred as of January 1, 2010. In addition, disclosure is required of any material nonrecurring transactions included in the pro forma adjustments.

Annual Report References

HUMANA 2010 ANNUAL REPORT

3. Acquisitions

On December 21, 2010, we acquired Concentra Inc., or Concentra, a health care company based in Addison, Texas, for cash consideration of $804.7 million. Through its affiliated clinicians, Concentra delivers occupational medicine, urgent care, physical therapy, and wellness services to workers and the general public through its operation of medical centers and worksite medical facilities. The Concentra acquisition provides entry into the primary care space on a national scale, offering additional means for achieving health and wellness solutions and providing an expandable platform for growth with a management team experienced in physician asset management and alternate site care. The preliminary fair values of Concentra's assets acquired and liabilities assumed at the date of the acquisition are summarized as follows:

(in thousands)	Concentra
Cash and cash equivalents	$ 21,317
Receivables	108,571
Other current assets	20,589
Property and equipment	131,837
Goodwill	531,372
Other intangible assets	188,000
Other long-term assets	12,935
Total assets acquired	1,014,621
Current liabilities	(100,091)
Other long-term liabilities	(109,811)
Total liabilities assumed	(209,902)
Net assets acquired	$ 804,719

The other intangible assets, which primarily consist of customer relationships and trade name, have a weighted average useful life of 13.7 years. Approximately $57.9 million of the acquired goodwill is deductible for tax purposes. The purchase price allocation is preliminary, subject to completion of valuation analyses, including, for example, refining assumptions used to calculate the fair value of other intangible assets. The purchase agreement contains provisions under which there may be future consideration paid or received related to the subsequent determination of working capital that existed at the acquisition date. Any payments or receipts for provisional amounts for working capital will be recorded as an adjustment to goodwill when paid or received.

The results of operations and financial condition of Concentra have been included in our consolidated statements of income and consolidated balance sheets from the acquisition date. In connection with the acquisition, we recognized approximately $14.9 million of acquisition-related costs, primarily banker and other professional fees, in selling, general and administrative expense. The pro forma financial information assuming the acquisition had occurred as of January 1, 2009 was not material to our results of operations.

On October 31, 2008, we acquired PHP Companies, Inc. (d/b/a Cariten Healthcare), or Cariten, for cash consideration of approximately $291.0 million, including the payment of $34.9 million during 2010 to settle a purchase price contingency. The Cariten acquisition increased our commercial fully-insured and ASO presence as well as our Medicare HMO presence in eastern Tennessee. During 2009, we continued our review of the fair value estimate of certain other intangible and net tangible assets acquired. This review resulted in a decrease of $27.1 million in the fair value of other intangible assets, primarily related to the fair value assigned to the customer contracts acquired. There was a corresponding adjustment to goodwill and deferred income taxes. The total consideration paid exceeded our estimated fair value of the net tangible assets acquired by approximately $145.8 million of which we allocated $52.3 million to other intangible assets and $93.5 million to goodwill. The other intangible assets, which primarily consist of customer contracts, have a weighted-average useful life of 11.6 years. The acquired goodwill is not deductible for tax purposes.

On August 29, 2008, we acquired Metcare Health Plans, Inc., or Metcare, for cash consideration of approximately $14.9 million. The acquisition expanded our Medicare HMO membership in central Florida.

On May 22, 2008, we acquired OSF Health Plans, Inc., or OSF, a managed care company serving both Medicare and commercial members in central Illinois, for cash consideration of approximately $87.3 million, including the payment of $3.3 million during 2009 to settle a purchase price contingency. This acquisition expanded our presence in Illinois, broadening our ability to serve multi-location employers with a wider range of products including our specialty offerings. The total consideration paid exceeded our estimated fair value of the net tangible assets acquired by approximately $31.1 million of which we allocated $10.1 million to other intangible assets and $21.0 million to goodwill. The other intangible assets, which primarily consist of customer contracts, have a weighted-average useful life of 9.9 years. The acquired goodwill is not deductible for tax purposes.

On April 30, 2008, we acquired UnitedHealth Group's Las Vegas, Nevada individual SecureHorizons Medicare Advantage HMO business, or SecureHorizons, for cash consideration of approximately $185.3 million, plus subsidiary capital and surplus requirements of $40 million. The acquisition expanded our presence in the Las Vegas market. The total consideration paid exceeded our estimated fair value of the net tangible assets acquired by approximately $185.3 million of which we allocated $69.3 million to other intangible assets and $116.0 million to goodwill. The other intangible assets, which primarily consist of customer contracts, have a weighted-average useful life of 10.9 years. The acquired goodwill is not deductible for tax purposes.

The purchase agreements for certain of the acquisitions discussed above occurring prior to January 1, 2009 contain provisions under which there may be future contingent consideration paid or received primarily associated with balance sheet settlements. Any contingent consideration paid or received will be recorded as an adjustment to goodwill when the contingencies are resolved. We do not expect these adjustments to be material.

The results of operations and financial condition of Cariten, Metcare, OSF, and SecureHorizons have been included in our consolidated statements of income and consolidated balance sheets since the acquisition dates.

Johnson Controls 2010 Annual Report

2. Acquisitions

In July 2010, the Company acquired an additional 40% of a power solutions Korean joint venture. The acquisition increased the Company's ownership percentage to 90%. The remaining 10% was acquired by the local management team. The Company paid approximately $86 million (excluding cash acquired of $57 million) for the additional ownership percentage and incurred approximately $10 million of acquisition costs and related purchase accounting adjustments. As a result of the acquisition, the Company recorded a non-cash gain of $47 million within power solutions equity income to adjust the Company's existing equity investment in the Korean joint venture to fair value. Goodwill of $51 million was recorded as part of the transaction. The purchase price allocation may be subsequently adjusted to reflect final valuation studies.

Also during fiscal 2010, the Company completed three acquisitions for a combined purchase price of $35 million, of which $32 million was paid as of September 30, 2010. The acquisitions in the aggregate were not material to the Company's consolidated financial statements. In connection with the acquisitions, the Company recorded goodwill of $9 million. The purchase price allocation may be subsequently adjusted to reflect final valuation studies.

During fiscal 2009, the Company completed four acquisitions for a combined purchase price of $43 million, of which $38 million was paid in the twelve months ended September 30, 2009. None of the acquisitions were material to the Company's consolidated financial statements. In connection with these acquisitions, the Company recorded goodwill of $30 million, of which $26 million was recorded during fiscal 2009.

In July 2008, the Company formed a joint venture to acquire the interior product assets of Plastech Engineered Products, Inc. (Plastech). Plastech filed for bankruptcy in February 2008. The Company owns 70% of the newly formed entity and certain Plastech term lenders hold the remaining noncontrolling interest. The Company contributed cash and injection molding plants to the new entity with a fair value of $262 million. The lenders contributed their rights to receive Plastech's interiors business obtained in exchange for certain Plastech debt. The combined equity in the new entity was approximately $375 million. Goodwill of $199 million was recorded as part of the transaction. In the third quarter of fiscal 2009, the Company finalized valuations associated with the acquisition and recorded a $21 million increase to goodwill.

Also in fiscal 2008, the Company completed seven additional acquisitions for a combined purchase price of $108 million, none of which were material to the Company's consolidated financial statements. In connection with these acquisitions, the Company recorded goodwill of $66 million.

Schlumberger NV 2010 Annual Report

4. Acquisitions

Merger with Smith International, Inc.

On August 27, 2010, Schlumberger acquired all of the outstanding shares of Smith, a leading supplier of premium products and services to the oil and gas exploration and production industry. The merger brings together the complementary drilling and measurements technologies and expertise of Schlumberger and Smith in order to facilitate the engineering of complete drilling systems which optimize all of the components of the drill string. Such systems will enable Schlumberger's customers to achieve improved drilling efficiency, better well placement and increased wellbore assurance as they face increasingly more challenging environments. In addition, Schlumberger's geographic footprint will facilitate the extension of joint offerings on a worldwide basis.

Under the terms of the merger agreement, Smith became a wholly-owned subsidiary of Schlumberger. Each share of Smith common stock issued and outstanding immediately prior to the effective time of the merger was converted into the right to receive 0.6966 shares of Schlumberger common stock, with cash paid in lieu of fractional shares.

At the effective time of the merger, each outstanding option to purchase Smith common stock was converted pursuant to the merger agreement into a stock option to acquire shares of Schlumberger common stock on the same terms and conditions as were in effect immediately prior to the completion of the merger. The number of shares of Schlumberger common stock underlying each converted Smith stock option was determined by multiplying the number of Smith stock options by the 0.6966 exchange ratio, and rounding down to the nearest whole share. The exercise price per share of each converted Smith stock option was determined by dividing the per share exercise price of such stock option by the 0.6966 exchange ratio, and rounded up to the nearest whole cent. Smith stock options, whether or not then vested and exercisable, became fully vested and exercisable and assumed by Schlumberger at the effective date of the merger in accordance with preexisting change-in-control provisions. Smith stock options were converted into 0.6 million of Schlumberger stock options.

At the effective time of the merger, Smith restricted stock units, whether or not then vested, became fully vested (except for grants between the date of the merger agreement and closing, which were not significant and did not automatically vest) and were converted into shares of Schlumberger common stock in connection with the merger, determined by multiplying the number of shares of Smith common stock subject to each award by the 0.6966 exchange ratio, rounded to the nearest whole share (assuming, in the case of performance-based Smith restricted stock unit awards, the deemed attainment of the performance goals under the award at the target level).

Calculation of Consideration Transferred

The following details the fair value of the consideration transferred to effect the merger with Smith.

(stated in millions, except exchange ratio and per share amounts)	
Number of shares of Smith common stock outstanding as of the acquisition date	248
Number of Smith unvested restricted stock units outstanding as of the acquisition date	4
	252
Multiplied by the exchange ratio	0.6966
Equivalent Schlumberger shares of common stock issued	176
Schlumberger closing stock price on August 27, 2010	$ 55.76
Common stock equity consideration	$ 9,812
Fair value of Schlumberger equivalent stock options issued	$ 16
Total fair value of the consideration transferred	$ 9,828

Certain amounts reflect rounding adjustments
Preliminary Allocation of Consideration Transferred to Net Assets
Acquired

The following amounts represent the preliminary estimates of the fair value of identifiable assets acquired and liabilities assumed in the merger. The final determination of fair value for certain assets and liabilities will be completed as soon as the information necessary to complete the analysis is obtained. These amounts will be finalized as soon as possible, but no later than one year from the acquisition date.

(stated in millions)

Cash	$ 399
Accounts receivable	1,831
Inventory[1]	2,013
Fixed assets	2,017
Intangible assets:	
Tradenames (weighted-average life of 25 years)	1,560
Technology (weighted-average life of 16 years)	1,170
Customer relationships (weighted average life of 23 years)	1,360
Other assets	429
Accounts payable and accrued liabilities	(1,460)
Long-term debt[2]	(2,141)
Deferred taxes[3]	(1,936)
Other liabilities	(528)
sub-total	$ 4,714
Less:	
Investment in M-I SWACO[4]	(1,429)
Noncontrolling interests	(111)
Total identifiable net assets	$ 3,174
Gain on investment in M-I SWACO[4]	(1,238)
Goodwill(5)	7,892
Total consideration transferred	$ 9,828

[1] Schlumberger recorded an adjustment of approximately $155 million to write-up the acquired inventory to its estimated fair value. Schlumberger's cost of revenue reflected this increased valuation as this inventory was sold. Accordingly, Schlumberger's margins were temporarily reduced in the initial periods subsequent to the merger.

(2) In connection with the merger, Schlumberger assumed all of the debt obligations of Smith including its long-term fixed rate notes consisting of the following: $220 million 6.75% Senior Notes due 2011, $300 million 8.625% Senior Notes due 2014, $275 million 6.00% Senior Notes due 2016 and $700 million 9.75% Senior Notes due 2019. Schlumberger recorded a $417 million adjustment to increase the carrying amount of these notes to their estimated fair value. This adjustment will be amortized as a reduction of interest expense over the remaining term of the respective obligations.

(3) In connection with the acquisition accounting, Schlumberger provided deferred taxes related to, among other items, the estimated fair value adjustments for acquired inventory, intangible assets and assumed debt obligations. Included in the provisions for deferred taxes are amounts relating to the outside basis difference associated with shares in certain Smith non-US subsidiaries for which no taxes have previously been provided. Schlumberger expects to reverse the outside basis difference primarily through the reorganization of those subsidiaries as well as through repatriating earnings in lieu of permanently reinvesting them. In this regard, Schlumberger is in the process of assessing certain factors that impact the ultimate amount of deferred taxes to be recorded. The amount of deferred taxes recorded will likely be revised after this assessment is completed. Any revision to the amount of deferred taxes recorded will impact the amount of goodwill recorded.

(4) Prior to the completion of the merger, Smith and Schlumberger operated M-I SWACO, a drilling fluids joint venture that was 40% owned by Schlumberger and 60% owned by Smith. Effective at the closing of the merger, M-I SWACO is now owned 100% by Schlumberger. As a result of obtaining control of this joint venture, Schlumberger was required under generally accepted accounting principles to remeasure its previously held equity interest in the joint venture at its merger-date fair value and recognize the resulting pretax gain of $1.3 billion ($1.2 billion after-tax) in earnings. This gain is classified as *Gain on Investment in M-I SWACO* in the *Consolidated Statement of Income*.

Prior to acquiring Smith, Schlumberger recorded income relating to this venture using the equity method of accounting. The carrying value of Schlumberger's investment in the joint venture on December 31, 2009 was $1.4 billion, and was included within *Investments in Affiliated Companies* on the *Consolidated Balance Sheet*. Schlumberger's equity income from this joint venture was $78 million in 2010 (representing the period from January 1, 2010 to August 27, 2010), $131 million in 2009 and $210 million in 2008.

Schlumberger received cash distributions from the joint venture of $50 million in 2010, $106 million in 2009 and $57 million in 2008.

(5) The goodwill recognized is primarily attributable to expected synergies that will result from combining the operations of Schlumberger and Smith as well as intangible assets that do not qualify for separate recognition. Approximately $0.2 billion of the goodwill is deductible for income tax purposes.

Acquisition of Geoservices

On April 23, 2010, Schlumberger completed the acquisition of Geoservices, a privately owned oilfield services company specializing in mud logging, slickline and production surveillance operations, for $915 million in cash.

The purchase price has been allocated to the net assets acquired upon their estimated fair values as follows:

(stated in millions)	
Cash	$ 26
Other assets	184
Fixed assets	90
Goodwill	599
Intangible assets	377
Long-term debt	(145)
Deferred tax liabilities	(64)
Other liabilities	(152)
	$ 915

The long-term debt was repaid at the time of closing.

Intangible assets recorded in connection with this transaction, which primarily relate to customer relationships, will be amortized over a weighted average period of approximately 17 years. The amount allocated to goodwill represents the excess of the purchase price over the fair value of the net assets acquired and is not tax deductible for income tax purposes.

Other Acquisitions

Schlumberger has made other acquisitions and minority investments, none of which were significant on an individual basis, for cash payments, net of cash acquired, of $212 million during 2010, $514 million during 2009, and $345 million during 2008.

Supplemental Pro Forma Data

Smith's results of operations have been included in Schlumberger's financial statements for periods subsequent to the effective date of the merger. Smith contributed revenues of $3.3 billion and net income of $160 million (including the recurring effects of purchase accounting) to Schlumberger for the period from the closing of the merger through December 31, 2010. The following unaudited supplemental pro forma data ("pro forma data") presents consolidated information as if the merger with Smith and the acquisition of Geoservices had been completed on January 1, 2009:

(stated in millions, except per share data)	2010	2009
Revenue	$ 33,468	$ 31,182
Net income	$ 3,376	$ 3,271
Net income attributable to Schlumberger	$ 3,370	$ 3,244
Diluted earnings per share	$ 2.44	$ 2.34

The pro forma data was prepared based on the historical financial information of Schlumberger, Smith and Geoservices and has been adjusted to give effect to pro forma adjustments that are (i) directly attributable to the transactions, (ii) factually supportable and (iii) expected to have a continuing impact on the combined results. The pro forma data is not necessarily indicative of what Schlumberger's results of operations actually would have been had the transactions been completed on January 1, 2009. Additionally, the pro forma data does not purport to project the future results of operations of the combined company nor do they reflect the expected realization of synergies associated with the transactions. The pro forma data reflects the application of the following adjustments:

- Elimination of the gain resulting from Schlumberger's remeasurement of its previously held 40% equity interest in M-I SWACO, which is considered non-recurring.
- Additional depreciation and amortization expense associated with fair value adjustments to acquired identifiable intangible assets and property, plant and equipment.
- Elimination of charges incurred in 2010 related to the fair value adjustments to Smith's inventory that has been sold as they will not have a long-term continuing impact.
- Reductions in interest expense as a result of increasing the carrying value of acquired debt obligations to its estimated fair value.

▶ Elimination of transaction costs incurred in 2010 that are directly related to the transactions, and do not have a continuing impact on the combined company's operating results.

▶ The issuance of 176 million of shares of Schlumberger common stock.

Included in the 2010 and 2009 pro forma net income attributable to Schlumberger and diluted earnings per share presented above are the following significant charges and credits:

(stated in millions, except per share data)	2010		2009	
	Net Income Impact	Diluted EPS Impact*	Net Income Impact	Diluted EPS Impact
Severance and other[1]	$ 77	$ 0.06	$ 85	$ 0.06
Impairment relating to WesternGeco's first generation Q-Land acquisition system[1]	71	0.05	-	-
Other WesternGeco-related charges[1]	63	0.05	-	-
Impact of elimination of tax deduction related to Medicare Part D subsidy[1]	40	0.03	-	-
Mexico restructuring[1]	36	0.03	-	-
Venezuelan currency-related losses[2]	35	0.03	-	-
Repurchase of bonds[1]	37	0.03	-	-
Gain on remeasurement of investment in @Balance[2]	(18)	(0.01)	-	-
Postretirement benefits curtailment[1]	-	-	122	0.09
Employee severance[2]	-	-	32	0.02
	$ 341	$ 0.25	$ 239	$ 0.17

* Does not add due to rounding

[1] Relates to Schlumberger's historical operations and is more fully described in Note 3 - *Charges and Credits*.

[2] Relates to Smith's historical operations.

17. Mergers, Acquisitions and Divestitures

Certain businesses were acquired for $1,214 million in cash and $114 million of liabilities assumed during 2008. These acquisitions were accounted for by the purchase method and, accordingly, results of operations have been included in the financial statements from their respective dates of acquisition.

The 2008 acquisitions included: Amic AB, a privately held Swedish developer of in vitro diagnostic technologies for use in point-of-care and near-patient settings; Beijing Dabao Cosmetics Co., Ltd., a company that sells personal care brands in China; SurgRx, Inc., a privately held developer of the advanced bipolar tissue sealing system used in the ENSEAL® family of devices; HealthMedia, Inc., a privately held company that creates webbased behavior change interventions; LGE Performance Systems, Inc., a privately held company known as Human Performance Institute™, which develops science-based training programs to improve employee engagement and productivity and Omrix Biopharmaceuticals, Inc., a fully integrated biopharmaceutical company that develops and markets biosurgical and immunotherapy products.

The excess of purchase price over the estimated fair value of tangible assets acquired amounted to $891 million and has been assigned to identifiable intangible assets, with any residual recorded to goodwill. Approximately $181 million has been identified as the value of IPR&D associated with the acquisitions of Omrix Biopharmaceuticals, Inc., Amic AB, SurgRx, Inc. and HealthMedia, Inc.

The IPR&D charge related to the acquisition of Omrix Biopharmaceuticals, Inc. was $127 million and is associated with stand-alone and combination biosurgical technologies used to achieve hemostasis. The value of the IPR&D was calculated using cash flow projections discounted for the risk inherent in such projects. Probability of success factors ranging from 60 -90% were used to reflect inherent clinical and regulatory risk. The discount rate applied was 14%. As of the end of the 2008 fiscal year, 97.8% of the outstanding shares of Common Stock of Omrix Biopharmaceuticals, Inc. had been tendered by stockholders. Excluding shares that were tendered subject to guaranteed delivery procedures, 90.2% of the outstanding shares of Common Stock had been tendered. On December 30, 2008 the Company completed the acquisition of Omrix Biopharmaceuticals, Inc.

The IPR&D charge related to the acquisition of Amic AB was $40 million and is associated with point-of-care device and 4CAST Chip technologies. The value of the IPR&D was calculated using cash flow projections discounted for the risk inherent in such projects. The discount rate applied was 20%.

The IPR&D charge related to the acquisition of SurgRx, Inc. was $7 million and is associated with vessel cutting and sealing surgical devices. The value of the IPR&D was calculated using cash flow projections discounted for the risk inherent in such projects. Probability of success factors ranging from 90 - 95% were used to reflect inherent clinical and regulatory risk. The discount rate applied was 18%.

The IPR&D charge related to the acquisition of HealthMedia, Inc. was $7 million and is associated primarily with process enhancements to software technology. The value of the IPR&D was calculated using cash flow projections discounted for the risk inherent in such projects. A probability of success factor of 90% was used to reflect inherent risk. The discount rate applied was 14%.

Certain businesses were acquired for $1,388 million in cash and $232 million of liabilities assumed during 2007. These acquisitions were accounted for by the purchase method and, accordingly, results of operations have been included in the financial statements from their respective dates of acquisition.

The 2007 acquisitions included: Conor Medsystems, Inc., a cardiovascular device company, with new drug delivery technology; Robert Reid, Inc., a Japanese orthopedic product distributor; and Maya's Mom, Inc., a social media company.

The excess of purchase price over the estimated fair value of tangible assets acquired amounted to $636 million and has been assigned to identifiable intangible assets, with any residual recorded to goodwill. Approximately $807 million has been identified as the value of IPR&D associated with the acquisition of Conor Medsystems, Inc.

The IPR&D charge related to the acquisition of Conor Medsystems, Inc. was $807 million and is associated with research related to the discovery and application of the stent technology. The value of the IPR&D was calculated using cash flow projections discounted for the risk inherent in such projects. The discount rate applied was 19%.

Certain businesses were acquired for $18.0 billion in cash and $1.3 billion of liabilities assumed during 2006. These acquisitions were accounted for by the purchase method and, accordingly, results of operations have been included in the financial statements from their respective dates of acquisition except as noted below.

On December 20, 2006, the Company completed the acquisition of the Consumer Healthcare business of Pfizer Inc. for a purchase price of $16.6 billion in cash. The operating results of the Consumer Healthcare business of Pfizer Inc. were reported in the Company's financial statements beginning in 2007, as 2006 results subsequent to the acquisition date were not significant. In order to obtain regulatory approval of the transaction, the Company agreed to divest certain overlapping businesses. The Company completed the divestiture of the ZANTAC® product on December 20, 2006 and the divestitures of KAOPECTATE®, UNISOM®, CORTIZONE®, BALMEX® and ACT® products on January 2, 2007.

The following table provides pro forma results of operations for the fiscal year ended December 31, 2006, as if the Consumer Healthcare business of Pfizer Inc. had been acquired as of the beginning of the period presented. The pro forma results include the effect of divestitures and certain purchase accounting adjustments such as the estimated changes in depreciation and amortization expense on the acquired tangible and intangible assets. However, pro forma results do not include any anticipated cost savings or other effects of the planned integration of the Consumer Healthcare business of Pfizer Inc. Accordingly, such amounts are not necessarily indicative of the results if the acquisition had occurred on the dates indicated or which may occur in the future.

(Unaudited)

(Shares in millions except per share data)	*Pro forma results Year ended December 31, 2006*
Net sales	$57,115
Net earnings	$10,770
Diluted net earnings per share	$ 3.64

The IPR&D charge related to the acquisition of the Consumer Healthcare business of Pfizer Inc. was $320 million on a pre-tax basis and $217 million on an after-tax basis and is primarily associated with rights obtained to the switch of ZYRTEC® from U.S. prescription to over-the-counter status. The switch was approved by the FDA effective November 2007. The value of the

IPR&D was calculated using cash flow projections discounted for the risk inherent in such projects. A probability of success factor of 95% was used to reflect inherent regulatory risk as of the acquisition date and the discount rate applied was 11%.

The Company completed the analysis of integration plans, pursuant to which the Company is incurring costs primarily related to the elimination of certain duplicate selling, general and administrative functions between the two companies in areas such as global business services, corporate staff and go-to-market support, as well as excess manufacturing capacity.

In addition to the acquisition of the Consumer Healthcare business of Pfizer Inc., 2006 acquisitions included: Animas Corporation, a leading maker of insulin infusion pumps and related products; Hand Innovations LLC, a privately held manufacturer of fracture fixation products for the upper extremities; Future Medical Systems S.A., a privately held company that primarily develops, manufactures and markets arthroscopic fluid management systems; Vascular Control Systems, Inc., a privately held company focused on developing medical devices to treat fibroids and to control bleeding in obstetric and gynecologic applications; Groupe Vendôme S.A., a privately held French marketer of adult and baby skin care products; ColBar LifeScience Ltd., a privately held company specializing in reconstructive medicine and tissue engineering and Ensure Medical, Inc., a privately held company that develops devices for postcatheterization closure of the femoral artery.

Excluding the acquisition of the Consumer Healthcare business of Pfizer Inc., the excess of purchase price over the estimated fair value of tangible assets acquired in 2006 amounted to $1,209 million and has been assigned to identifiable intangible assets, with any residual recorded to goodwill. Approximately $239 million has been identified as the value of IPR&D primarily associated with the acquisitions of Hand Innovations LLC, Future Medical Systems S.A., Vascular Control Systems, Inc., ColBar LifeScience Ltd. and Ensure Medical, Inc.

The IPR&D charge related to the acquisition of Hand Innovations LLC was $22 million and is associated with fracture repair technologies. The value of the IPR&D was calculated using cash flow projections discounted for the risk inherent in such projects. Probability of success factors ranging from 38 - 95% were used to reflect inherent clinical and regulatory risk and the discount rate applied was 17%.

The IPR&D charge related to the acquisition of Future Medical Systems S.A. was $15 million and is associated with the NEXTRA and DUO PUMP product technologies. The value of the IPR&D was calculated using cash flow projections discounted for the risk inherent in such projects. A probability of success factor of 90% for both technologies was used to reflect inherent clinical and regulatory risk and the discount rate applied was 22%.

The IPR&D charge related to the acquisition of Vascular Control Systems, Inc. was $87 million and is associated with the FLOSTAT system technology. The value of the IPR&D was calculated using cash flow projections discounted for the risk inherent in such projects. A probability of success factor of 75% was used to reflect inherent clinical and regulatory risk and the discount rate applied was 21%.

The IPR&D charge related to the acquisition of ColBar LifeScience Ltd. was $49 million and is associated with the EVOLENCE® family of products, which are biodegradable dermal fillers. The value of the IPR&D was calculated using cash flow projections discounted for the risk inherent in such projects. Probability of success factors ranging from 70-80% were used to reflect inherent clinical and regulatory risk and the discount rate applied was 21%.

The IPR&D charge related to the acquisition of Ensure Medical, Inc. was $66 million and is associated with the femoral artery closure device. The value of the IPR&D was calculated using cash flow projections discounted for the risk inherent in such projects. A probability of success factor of 75% was used to reflect inherent clinical and regulatory risk and the discount rate applied was 22%.

With the exception of the Consumer Healthcare business of Pfizer Inc., supplemental pro forma information for 2008, 2007 and 2006 per SFAS No. 141, *Business Combinations,* and SFAS No. 142, *Goodwill and Other Intangible Assets,* is not provided, as the impact of the aforementioned acquisitions did not have a material effect on the Company's results of operations, cash flows or financial position.

With the exception of the divestiture of the Professional Wound Care business of Ethicon, Inc., which resulted in a gain of $536 million before tax, and is recorded in other (income) expense, net, in 2008, divestitures in 2008, 2007 and 2006 did not have a material effect on the Company's results of operations, cash flows or financial position.

Financial Statement Analysis of Business Combination

Acquisitions must be analyzed, especially by examining footnote disclosures, because they can create an appearance of earnings and growth when they are not really present.

For analytical purposes, net income should be downwardly adjusted for the difference between reported gain and what the gain would have been if the assets were valued at fair market value.

The analyst must carefully scrutinize disclosures relating to deriving fair market values of the assets and liabilities of the acquired company. He must ascertain the reasonableness of such valuations.

If equity securities are involved in the purchase transaction, the analyst should determine whether the market prices of the securities were unusually high at the transaction date. If so, net assets will be inflated due to the temporary ceiling market prices. In this case, the analyst may wish to use the average market price of the securities for his own valuation of the acquired assets.

The analyst must be alert to the possible overstatement of estimated liabilities for future costs and losses that may increase postacquisition earnings.

Emergence of Corporate Development officers (CDOs)—In-House M&A Teams

According to a 2004 study by Ernst & Young, a new class of executive is emerging in North America, potentially encroaching on the advisory role traditionally played by investment bankers. Corporate development officers (CDOs), or the heads of in-house merger and acquisition teams, are gaining more power and influence in the wake of US corporate governance reforms.

The change is being driven by CEOs' concerns about the risks associated with bad deals. CFOs need to spend their time mostly on complying with new legislation's stricter reporting rules. The big shift here is that in today's environment the focus is really on ensuring there is somebody at the executive level that has responsibility for the life of a deal. Symantec, the security software maker, and Honeywell, the engineering group, have recently bolstered the roles of their CDOs. The E&Y study is based on interviews with 175 US and Canadian executives responsible for corporate development, including 26 from Fortune 100 companies. Some observers suggest the presence of a senior executive dedicated solely to deal-making might mean that external advisers such as investment banks lose significant amounts of business.

The study has reignited worries that advisory work by Wall Street firms is becoming commoditized. If the strategic thinking on mergers and acquisitions deals that generate high fees is being done within companies, they will turn to banks only for lower fee-paying execution work, the argument goes. Large companies such as General Electric with well-staffed in-house corporate development teams have never shied away from extensive use of investment bankers for M&A as well.

A caveat: Some fundamental parts of a deal still require the presence of an independent financial adviser. There is the need for an independent valuation, the ability to engage in tough negotiations without damaging relationships and a complete understanding of how competitors might react.

Making a corporate marriage work

Bringing two companies together is an enormous task. There are grand, big- picture questions that need to be resolved, such as the new group's strategy and direction. There are also administrative, logistical and technical challenges. Will new contracts of employment be required? Where should the headquarters of the combined operation be located? How can the companies' information technology systems be integrated? Below is a list of steps to be addressed:

▶ Should you be starting from here? Are there compelling strategic reasons for this deal? Or is the company under pressure from investors and the media? Is the CEO looking for a last hurrah before moving on?

▶ Get your integration right. Set target dates for major decisions on structure.

▶ Define the key functions in the new entity—including finance, HR, IT, legal—as soon as you can.

▶ Plan to resolve cultural differences; this will largely happen through good communication.

▶ Be careful to give customers priority during the transition; employees will not be the only stakeholders feeling unsettled.

Conclusion

Generally, a company does not acquire another business unless it is a growing, successful company. In analyzing a potential merger and acquisition, many considerations must be taken into account, such as the market price of stock, earnings per share, dividends, book value of assets, risk, and tax considerations.

CHAPTER 2

Divestiture

Unbundling

Unbundling is often understood as what happens when a company disposes of or sells assets, facilities, product lines, subsidiaries, divisions or business units. An unbundling operation is an alteration to a company's productive portfolio through the disposal or sale of a division, a business unit, a product line or a subsidiary. Unbundling is discussed in terms of divestments and divestitures. These terms are often used as synonyms, but they are, in fact, distinct strategic options. A divestment is the partial or complete sale or disposal of physical and organizational assets, the closing of facilities and the reduction of the workforce. A divestiture, on the other hand, is the partial or complete sale or disposal of a business unit, product line, subsidiary or division. It is only with a divestiture, and not with a divestment, that the parent organization creates a new company, able to operate more or less autonomously in the market. It is important to understand that unbundling operations are more than just financing operations. Their design and implementation affect the success of the parent company and the divested unit, from both a financial and a strategic perspective.

The divestiture of business segments by corporations has become an accepted strategy for growth rather than diversification. Divestiture involves the partial or complete conversion, disposition and reallocation of people, money, inventories, plants, equipment and products. It is the process of eliminating a portion of the enterprise for subsequent use of the freed resources for some other purpose. A divestment may involve a manufacturing, marketing, research or other business function.

A business segment may be subject to divestiture if they:

1. Do not produce an acceptable return on invested capital.
2. Do not generate sufficient cash flow.
3. Fit in with the overall corporate strategy.
4. Are unrelated to their primary lines of business.
5. Fail to meet management goals for growth in profits, sales or in other respects.
6. The worth of the pieces is greater than that of the whole.

Corrective divestitures are intended to correct strategic mistakes. They aim to reduce over-diversification, refocus on core businesses, eliminate negative synergies or realign corporate strategy with the company's identity. Divestiture first appears in the early stages of the downturn, as corporations needed cash. Many dynamic, fast-growing companies are combining with slower growing, mature companies to produce a more diversified corporate portfolio. However, during this time many companies find that if you have too many businesses it spreads the cash too thin. Also, this random mixture of businesses under one corporate umbrella causes a great deal of concern among the financial industry. This mix makes it difficult to measure actual segment performance.

In 1976, the Securities and Exchange Commission persuaded the Financial Accounting Standards Board (FASB) that publicly held companies should report the assets held and income generated by disaggregated corporate segments of similar products and services. Thus, for the first time the public found out that many of a company's business segments were unprofitable! This disclosure forced management to explain to the shareholders why certain segments of the corporation were producing such low returns on the stockholder's invested capital. For the first time, corporate executives were forced into developing divestiture strategies to eliminate the unprofitable section of the business.

Resource allocation becomes an important consideration in a diversified business. These resources are not only capital but also include management talent. If management finds itself spending an excessive amount of time and energy on one segment of the corporation, that segment may be a candidate for divestiture. Then those resources can be redirected to the growing segments of the business. However, this operation also requires the attention of management.

Objectives and Types of Divestitures

Sooner or later a corporation will find itself in the position of needing to divest some of its assets. This may be for a variety of reasons. The usual objectives behind divestiture are to reposition the company in a market, raise cash, and to reduce losses. The other alternatives to divestiture are liquidation and bankruptcy; however, in this time of acquisitions and buyouts usually a buyer can be found for the other guy's dog. There are four primary types of divestitures:

(a) Sale of an operating unit to another firm
(b) Discharge of the managers of the unit being divested
(c) Setting up the business to be divested as a separate corporation and then giving (or "spinning off") its stock to the divesting firm's stockholders on a pro rata basis
(d) Outright liquidation of assets

When the divestiture is in the form of a sale to another firm, it usually involves an entire division or unit and is generally for cash but sometimes for stock of the acquiring firm. In a managerial buyout, the division managers themselves purchase the division, often through a leverage buyout (LBO), and reorganize it as a closely held firm. In a *spin-off*, the firm's existing stockholders are given new stock representing separate ownership in the company that was divested. The new company establishes its own board of directors and officers and operates as a separate entity. A spin-off is a type of restructuring that is characterized by establishing a new and separate entity and transferring its newly issued stock to the shareholders of the original company. It is accomplished by distributing a property dividend in the form of stock of another corporation to shareholders, who then become shareholders of both corporations. In *liquidation*, the assets of the divested unit are sold off separately instead of as a whole.

Reasons for Divestiture

Prior to formulating a divestiture strategy and determining which segments should be divested, the reasons for divestiture need to be listed. Exhibit 3 summarizes the reasons given by management for divesting segments of their business.

Exhibit 3: Reasons Managers Cite for Divesting Segments of their Business

	Frequency Given
Poor Performance	26%
Changes in Plans	23%
Excessive Resource Needs	19%
Constraints in Operation	15%
Source of Funds	10%
Antitrust	7%
	100%

As a result of the FASB decision in FASB No. 14 regarding the reporting of each business segment's operating costs and whether a profit is made or not, corporate management has been less reluctant to hold on to poorly performing business segments. However, there may be a logical reason to keep a poorly performing segment, such as an expected turn around, or the unit provides components or services to another unit with the company.

A diversified decision may result after the corporation has reviewed its operational philosophy and overall business strategy (whether this reevaluation was voluntary or forced by environment changes), and found business segments that no longer fit into the corporate image or are a business the company does not want to be involved in any more. An example of this is Schering-Plough's attempt to sell its Maybelline Cosmetics Division to concentrate resources and time on their more profitable prescription and consumer drug businesses. This restructuring will allow Schering-Plough to earn more on its invested capital. Operating margins for drugs are near 24%, which is more than twice that of the Maybelline Division.

The need to raise cash to pay off debt resulting from operations or acquisition/ diversification is another frequent reason for selling off a segment of the corporation. In this case though, many times the segment being sold is a winner. By selling a winning segment the company may hope to put itself on firmer financial ground by reducing debt. In this case where the company is trying to raise cash, the best segment to sell is the one that would require the least work to sell and bring in the greatest amount of cash over book value. For example, if a company had two divisions, a retail operation and the other which builds and leases railcars, and the sale of either would make a significant dent in the company's debt load, which division should be sold? The retail should be sold because the market for that type of operation is much better than for railcars.

There are other less common reasons such as personality conflicts among division management and that of the parent company or government decree or public outcry as in the case of many companies that had dealings in South Africa. On a rare occasion, the company may actually be approached and asked if they would be willing to sell the business.

Determining What Areas/Units Should be Sold

When trying to determine which areas or units of the company could be sold off, there are some simple guidelines that management should follow:

- The sum of a division's parts may be greater in value than the whole division;
- Simple components of a division may be sold more easily than the whole division itself;
- The disposal of a corporate division is a major marketing operation;
- Planning should include an evaluation from the viewpoint of the potential buyer;
- A spin-off should be considered if the division is large enough and may be potentially publicly traded.

In addition, management must review existing operations and identify those divisions that don't relate to the primary focus of the company or don't meet internal financial and performance standards. Special strength of each division must also be considered. Does a division provide a unique service, have a special marketing, distribution system or production facilities that may be of more value to another company? Also, the financial aspects must be considered. The historical and projected return on investment needs to be calculated and tabulated for each division.

Using these guidelines and the information determined above, management can focus on three topics. First, the attractiveness and value to others versus the arguments for keeping the division. Secondly, what corrective action would need to be taken to make the division a keeper. Thirdly, the current value of the division to the company. Only after considering all of these factors can a divestiture decision be made for a division.

Divestiture or Restructuring Planning

Planning for divestitures, as for acquisitions, should be related to the company's overall objectives and long-range plans. Typically, this process requires that management:

- Review existing operations — Identify those lines that either do not relate to primary product areas or do not meet internal financial and operating goals. Special strengths and weaknesses should be inventoried. These might include, for example, the existence (or absence) of special marketing, distribution, or product facilities that might be more valuable to another company
- Calculate each operating unit's historical and projected return on investment (historical and current value) and profit contributions.
- Determine what units are to be divested —Using the information obtained in the steps above, study high-priority divestiture possibilities. Focus on (1) the attractiveness and value to others vs. the arguments for retention, (2) corrective action that might be taken and (3) the current value to the company. Only then should a decision be made about which units, if any, to divest.
- Identify logical acquirers — Identify companies, groups, or individuals for whom the particular strengths of a unit to be divested would be of most value as well as the weaknesses that would be of least concern. Consideration should also be given to selling a unit to management through a leveraged buyout or to employees through an Employee Stock Ownership Plan (ESOP).

The use of these techniques allows employees to become owners of the divested unit and thereby helps ensure their continued employment.

Sale Planning

Selling a business is one of the most difficult decisions that management and stockholders face. In the case of publicly owned companies, the decision process is similar to that noted above for acquisition and divestiture planning. In particular the following considerations need to be addressed:

▶ The company's present position and outlook compared with its long-term goals and objectives.

▶ Its capabilities for overcoming likely obstacles or threats, and its ability to capitalize on expected opportunities and accomplish long-term goals and objectives.

▶ Its market value in relation to underlying intrinsic or expected value.

▶ Its value to others (likely to be realized only through merger) in relation to present market value.

▶ Alternative approaches to realizing intrinsic value if it is higher than current market value.

▶ The outlook for the business and reinvestment opportunities compared with the stock market's perception of these factors.

In evaluating the company's present position, outlook and capabilities, the following questions need to be asked:

▶ Is the company and/or its products nearing *maturity,* thereby indicating that stockholder value might be maximized by sale in the near future? (Note: Studies show that maximum value is achieved through sale while revenues and *profits* are still growing at, or above, their historical rates.?

▶ Is the company's industry nearing a mature stage?

▶ Will some form of corporate development activity (e.g., acquisition, new product development, joint venture, marketing arrangements) be required to penetrate the company's markets beyond current levels?

▶ Are the company's products likely to lose their uniqueness in the near future, and/or is the company unable to make the commitment necessary to maintain the uniqueness of its products?

▶ Is the company's market stable or declining? Are capital requirements likely to be a drain on the company in the future due to aging facilities, rapidly growing sales and/or industry, changing technology or increasing competition?

▶ Is the company finding it difficult to obtain raw materials or labor at competitive prices?

▶ Is the company's performance (based on key financial ratios) behind the industry norm, or is it declining relative to the rest of the industry?

- Is competition likely to increase in the near future?
- Is management lacking in depth, experience or capability when compared with the rest of the industry?
- Does the company have excess capacity that is unlikely to be filled in the near future?
- Is the company lacking a well-defined strategy for future growth and profitability?
- Is management/employee morale waning for any reason?
- Is the company worth more to others than to current stockholders (i.e., are there potential buyers that can maximize potential quicker than the current stockholders can)? How saleable is the business?
- Will a sale really accomplish the business objectives of the company? Are there better alternatives?

Needless to say, making the decision requires complete objectivity on the part of both privately owned and publicly owned companies. Privately owned companies, however, must also consider the personal objectives of stockholders, whether or not they are active in the business. The questions below are designed to help those stockholders weigh various personal considerations that generally enter into a decision to sell or not sell. These personal considerations, of course, must be evaluated together with the business considerations already noted above:

- Are stockholders who are active in the business also approaching retirement age?
- Does the company have a competent manager to assume leadership of the business upon retirement or death of active stockholders?
- Do the stockholders need to create personal liquidity (for retirement, estate taxes, lifestyle or other reasons) or to diversify investment risk?
- Are there other personal considerations (e.g., personal or family health problems, marital difficulties, family disagreements, disagreements with other stockholders or with management, age, boredom, commitments to philanthropic, civic, leisure and other business activities) that would cause stockholders to consider a sale or that might make them less effective in running the business?
- Will a sale really accomplish the personal objectives of the stockholders? Are there better alternatives?
- What is the value of the business to current stockholders if intangible personal considerations are included compared with its value to others?

Once a decision to sell has been made, in-depth planning should begin. Answers to the following questions should help management and/or stockholders with that planning:

▶ Have you exploited the strengths of the business and done all you can to minimize the weaknesses?

▶ Have you estimated the worth of the business vs. its worth in the future?

▶ Is the timing right for achieving maximum value?

▶ Do you know the tax ramifications of the sale?

▶ What form of transaction best satisfies the business objectives and, in the case of privately held companies, the personal objectives of stockholders?

▶ Has adequate information been assembled to present to potential buyers?

▶ Who are the logical buyers?

▶ Have you developed an effective plan to identify and approach those buyers?

▶ Should you involve an investment banker or merger and acquisition consultant? How should the consultant be chosen and compensated? (Note: Generally, such an adviser should be engaged).

▶ Do you have a plan to deal with interested buyers, employees, customers and others during the sale process?

▶ Are there other details that need to be nailed down?

It is particularly important to do everything that can be done to increase the attractiveness of the business prior to sale, such as divesting undesirable assets or improving profitability. It's also important to anticipate the information potential buyers will want and the questions they will ask. A few final questions should also be answered before marketing of the company begins:

▶ Have all possible buyers been identified, not just the most probable ones?

▶ How will marketing of the company to possible buyers and inquiries be handled?

▶ Have pricing strategies been developed?

▶ Have negotiating strategies been developed?

▶ Has consideration been given on how to structure the transaction from a financial viewpoint (and a tax and accounting viewpoint as well)?

▶ Have acceptable forms of financing the transaction by the buyer been considered?

▶ Have alternative selling strategies been considered?

In summary, management should design an acquisition, divestiture or sale program that identifies major issues and opportunities, analyzes alternatives, fixes responsibility for performance and monitors progress. This overview is intended only to suggest the basic steps involved in acquisition, divestiture and sale planning; each company embarking on such a program should develop a planning system that meets its own special requirements.

Employee Considerations

Once the decision to divest a division has been made, there are two approaches to dealing with employees. The first, and least often done, is to be up front and tell them that the division is for sale. This can result in a variety of negative responses. The employees' morale may further deteriorate. (usually the morale is already poor because the division is not doing well). Or worse, the employees' may engage in a job action. The employees can also be a potential source of a buy-out of the company so unless the upper management is very aware with the employees' attitude the decision to tell or not is a difficult one. Another tactic is for management to tell the employees that the division is being sold and offer incentive bonuses to all employees who stay on through the divestiture and following acquisition.

Typically though, the parent company will form a senior management team whose sole function is to divest the division, occasionally even the top management of the division being divested doesn't know it is being sold. There are some reasons behind choosing an upper management team to do the divestiture. First, companies tend to divest in secret. Any leak of the news could cause any of the employee problems mentioned above. This is especially true in the case where finding a buyer may take a long time. (a longer time means more likelihood for a leak). Secondly, the head of a division is never the right person to sell the division. No matter how the decision to divest is sugar coated it is still an admission of failure. This makes it difficult for the managers to take an objective view of the business. It also impedes the decision on who is a suitable and qualified buyer of the company. Having the management team doing the divestiture also avoids or minimizes any conflict between those who may be responsible for the failure and those who were not. The third reason to appoint a top management team to do the divestiture is that it is simply not a job that would be welcomed by lower level managers. It is a thankless task that brings little reward for a hard job well done and has no future. It is a dead-end job!

Because the job falls on senior management, this also creates a problem. Their time is limited, particularly during a period where the company is trying to recover. If the team has little time nor the inclination to do this divestiture, the job performed may be sloppy. The decision analysis could be approximate rather than one based on actual numbers, as may be the selling price.

Also, if pressed for time the team may be restricted to dealing with only one buyer instead of negotiating with many suitors, which will improve the selling price and the return for the parent. This time pressure may be caused by the division's cash requirements rather than the divestiture team time constraints. If the parent can only support the cash drain of the division for a certain time period after the decision to divest, this puts a definite time constraint on the timing of the sale.

Means of Divestiture

After the initial planning of the divestiture, comes the tricky part of approaching potential buyers. The trick involved is to present enough information to peak the interest but also present the need for confidentiality (if required by the situation). The usual technique is to sound out a few potential buyers at a time, to see if they would be interested in acquiring a business in your industry with sales potential of X dollars.

This is done by sending out a short letter or a phone call to the CEO of the possibly interested firms. This communication again should just wet their appetite for information. If they express a desire for further dialogue, a prospectus should be sent. However, if after reviewing the prospectus and no further interest exist, this potential acquirer should be crossed off the list.

The other option depending on the skills and time demands of the members of the divestiture team is to use a third party (broker) to find suitable buyers and enter into negotiations. The use of the third party will in many cases provide a veil of secrecy, if needed. The third party is also useful in trying to market the division on a worldwide scale. This can get exposure for the division, which is particularly important where the parent or division had no previous exposure.

Valuation and Appraisal in Divestiture

When the time comes to sell a division, an asking price needs to be determined. Valuation of a division is not an exact science, and in the final analysis the value of a division is in the eye of the purchaser. While the expertise of an investment banker or business broker can and should be enlisted in setting the price of the division there are some standard accounting methods that can be used to estimate a division's value. A business broker will usually be very willing to help in the initial estimate phase in hopes that they will get the opportunity to act as your agent in selling the division. These valuation methods will be broken down into asset valuation methods, those based on sales and income, and those based on market comparisons. Although these methods vary in their applicability and depend on certain facts and circumstances they can be used to determine a range of values for a division.

There are basically four groups of methods of valuation or appraisal: (1) asset valuation methods, (2) sales and income methods, (3) market comparison methods, and (4) discounted cash flow methods.

Asset Valuation Methods

Asset valuation methods are based on the asset value of a business segment. Four popular methods are described below.

Adjusted Net Book Value

One of the most conservative methods of valuation is the adjusted net book value, because it determines the value based on historical (book) value and not on market value. This can be adjusted to compensate for this shortage by adding in such items as favorable lease arrangements, and other intangible items such as customer lists, patents, and goodwill.

Replacement Cost

Another method is the replacement cost technique. It asks, "What would it cost to purchase the division's assets new?" This method will give a higher division value than the adjusted net book value method and is therefore good for adjusting the book value to account for new costs. This figure can also be used as a basis for determining the liquidation value of the division's assets. The most reasonable value comes from adjusting the replacement value for depreciation and obsolescence of equipment.

Liquidation Value

The liquidation value is also a conservative estimate of a division's value since it does not consider the division's ongoing earning power. The liquidation value does provide the seller with a bottom line figure as to how low the price can be. The liquidation value is determined by estimating the cash value of assets assuming that they are to be sold in a short period of time. All the liabilities, real and estimated, are then deducted from the cash that was raised to determine the net liquidation value. Liquidation value can be determined based on fire sale prices or on a longer-term sales price. Obviously, the fire sale value would be lower.

Secured Loan Value

The secured loan value technique is based on the borrowing power of the division's assets. Banks will usually lend up to 90% of the value of accounts receivable and anywhere from 10-60% on the value of inventory depending on the quantity of the inventory in the conversion process.

Sales and Income Factors

Using sales and/or income figures as the basis for valuation can be made in two different ways.

Price-Earnings (P-E) Ratios

The P-E ratio for publicly held companies is known and therefore valuation is made easy. The division's value can be determined by multiplying the P-E ratio by the expected earnings for the division. This will give a derived price that all suitors can readily understand. The earnings can be estimated from quarterly or annual reports published by the company.

For privately held companies, however, it is difficult to determine a P-E ratio as the stock of the company is not traded and the earnings are rarely disclosed. However, the earnings can be estimated and an industry average P-E ratio can be used in the calculation to estimate the private company's sales value.

Sales or Earnings Multiples

There are many rules of thumb that can be used when estimating a division's value based on a multiple of sales or earnings. For example, insurance agencies sell for 200% of annual commissions or liquor stores sell for 10 times monthly sales. Another example would be radio stations selling for 8 times earnings or cash flow. These rules are fast and dirty and may result in a completely erroneous estimate of a division's value. Most business brokers will know these rule of thumb values to assist management in estimating the value of a division.

Market-based Comparisons

Every day that a public company is traded on the stock market a new value is assigned to it by the traders. Thus, the stock price can be compared to equivalent companies, in terms of products, size of operations, and average P-E ratios. From these P-E ratios, an estimated sales price can be estimated as described earlier.

In the case of private companies, it is difficult for the buyer to determine the earnings of the company. However, they can compare the company to other companies that are publicly traded. Comparison to publicly traded companies is necessary as the sales price is typically disclosed in the sale or acquisition announcement.

Discounted Cash Flow Analysis

Another method of determining value of a business segment is to use discounted cash flow (DCF) analysis. This bases the value of the segment on the current value of its projected cash flow. In theory, this method should result in a division's value being equal to that determined by one of the P-E ratio calculations, since both reflect the current worth of the company's earnings. In actuality, discounted cash flow is basing the value of the company on actual forecasted cash flows whereas the stock market is basing the stock price on other things including the markets perception of the company and its potential cash flow.

The DCF method requires information on:
- Forecasted actual cash flows.
- Assumed terminal (residual) value of the division at the end of the forecast period (book value, zero, or a multiple of earnings are frequently used).
- Discount rate. Choosing the right discount rate is the key to the successful use of the DCF technique. It must take into account the following factors:
- Purchaser's expected return on investment (ROI)
- Purchaser's assessment of risk
- Cost of capital
- Projected inflation rates
- Current interest rates

In general, whichever method of evaluation is chosen it is wise to check that resulting value with at least one other method to see if it is a reasonable figure. We have to be careful of excessively high or low figures. It is also a good idea to determine the liquidation value of the company or division, as this will set a *floor* for negotiations.

An Illustration: Discounted Cash Flow Analysis

Management will choose to divest a segment of their business if they perceive that the action will increase the wealth of the stockholders, as reflected in the price of the firm's stock. It can be further said that the price of the firm's stock will react favorably to a divestiture if the new present value of the transaction is perceived by the market to be positive.

Should a profitable business segment be retained and not divested, it would generate annual cash inflows for a particular or infinite number of years. Discounted cash flow analysis involves a comparison of initial incoming cash flows resulting from the sale of a business unit with the present value of the foregone future cash inflows given up by the firm. Foregone future cash flows refer to the cash flows that the business unit is anticipated to generate and will do so for the acquiring firm. The divesting firm gives up these cash inflows in exchange for the selling price of the business segment. For divestiture analysis to be of any value, the foregone future cash flow must be accurately estimated. The present value of these future inflows are found by discounting them at the firm's weighted average cost of capital, k.

Example 27

Exhibit 4 shows estimated cash inflows and outflows for a fictitious divestment candidate (FDC) over the next five years. The cash flows represent the best estimates by the managers of FDC's parent company and they further believe that FDC will be able to be sold at its residual value of $58.7 million in five years.

The firm's cost of capital is assumed to be known and is 15%.

The net present value of the future cash inflows of FDC is $47.26 million. If FDC were to be divested, the managers of its parent company should only consider selling prices greater than this amount. This logic also assumes that the $47.3 million can be reinvested at a 15% rate of return.

Another way of looking at this valuing task makes use of the following equation for divestiture net present value (DNPV):

$$DNPV = I - \sum \frac{NCF_t}{(1 + k)^t} \quad (1)$$

where I = the selling price of the business unit and NCF_t = net cash flow in period t. If a $50 million offer was made by a firm for FDC, the DNPV from Equation 1 will equal $2.7 million, as shown below.

$$DNPV = 50 - \frac{9.8}{1.15} + \frac{3.4}{1.15^2} + \frac{2.4}{1.15^3} + \frac{5.8}{1.15^4} + \frac{62.9}{1.15^5}$$

DNPV = $50 - $47.26 = $ 2.74 Million.

Exhibit 4

FDC's Cash Flow Projections (in Millions)

Cash Inflows	1	2	3	4	5
Net Operating Profit	$ 3.10	$ 3.60	$ 4.00	$ 5.10	$ 6.00
Depreciation	2.1	2.4	1.8	2.3	2.1
Residual Value					58.7
Total	$ 5.20	$ 6.00	$ 5.80	$ 7.40	$ 66.80

Cash Outflows					
Capital Expenditure	$ 1.70	$ 1.30	$ 0.80	$ 2.10	$ 1.70
Increase (Decrease)					
in working Capital	-6.3	1.3	2.6	-0.5	2.2
Total	-$4.60	$2.60	$3.40	$1.60	$3.90
Net Cash Inflow (NCF)	$ 9.80	$ 3.40	$ 2.40	$ 5.80	$ 62.90
Present value of $1*	0.8696	0.7561	0.6575	0.5718	0.4972
Present Value	$8.52	$2.57	$1.58	$3.32	$31.27
Total present value	$47.26				

* Note: Table 1 = Present value interest factor for the cost of capital of 15%.

From a financial point of view, this divestment is acceptable. If the divestment candidate has an unlimited life, such as a division in a healthy industry, then cash flows must be forecasted to infinity. This task is made simple by treating the cash flows similarly to a constant growth stock and value accordingly. If the cash inflows are expected to remain constant (zero growth) to infinity, than the present value of the NCF can be determined in the same manner as for a preferred stock, or perpetuity. In this case, the DNPV will be

$$DNPV = I - \frac{NCF}{k} \quad (2)$$

For future cash flows that are expected to grow at an after tax rate of g, the present value of those flows can be found using the constant growth valuation model. In this case, the DNPV will be

$$DNPV = I - \frac{NCF_1}{k - g} \quad (3)$$

where NCF1 = the expected NCF in the next period.

A final situation encountered often when evaluating divestiture candidates is the case where the NCFs are expected to be uneven for a number of years followed by even growth. In this case, the DNPV can be found as

$$DNPV = I - \frac{NCF_1}{(1+k)^1} + \frac{NCF_2}{(1+k)^2} + ... + \frac{NCF_{c-1}}{(k-g)} \times \frac{1}{(1 + k)}$$

where NCF1 and NCF2 represent foregone cash flows in periods 1 and 2 and c = the first year in which constant growth applies.

103

Firms should only divest of assets with positive DNPVs. To do so will increase the value of the firm and subsequently, the price of its stock. If two different candidates are mutually exclusive, the one with the highest DNPV should be chosen since this will increase the value of the firm the most. If divestiture is forced by the government, for example, and the firm finds it has a choice of candidates, all with negative DNPVs, it should divest the one whose DNPV is closest to zero, since this will reduce the value of the firm the least.

Divestiture with Uncertainty

Due to the difficulty in predicting the NCFs and also in knowing what kinds of prices will be offered for the divestment candidate, the divestment's net present value is normally uncertain.

For situations involving an unknown selling price (due to a lack of offers) the parent firm can either elect not to divest of the candidate or set its asking price such that the DNPV will equal zero. This should be the minimum they are willing to accept. They can also look for other divestment candidates that offer promising DNPVs.

Adjusting for uncertain NCFs is much more difficult and while there is no generally accepted method for accounting for this risk, there are a number of useful techniques that are borrowed from capital budgeting and can be used here.

Risk Adjusted Discount Rate

Employing a risk-adjusted discount rate is one technique that can be used to account for the uncertainty of the expected NCFs. In the previous examples, the firm's weighted average cost of capital was used to discount the NCFs to their present value. This is an appropriate choice when the divestiture candidate is as risky as the firm itself. When it is more risky, the use of a higher discount rate can be used for adjustment. This will reduce the present values of the cash flows and increase the DNPV. This is logical since a relatively risky divestment candidate with uncertain cash flows will be of less value to the firm, in present dollars. The added benefit of divesting such a candidate will be reflected in the increased DNPV. On the other hand, when the NCFs are more certain than those of the rest of the firm, the discount rate should be lowered. This lowers the DNPV and makes the divestiture less attractive. Equation 1 can be rewritten as shown below:

$$DNPV = I - \sum \frac{NCF_t}{(1 + k')^t}$$

where all terms are the same except for k' which now is the adjusted rate to be used for discounting the cash flows. Using data from Table 2 and assuming that the divestment candidate is less risky than the firm as a whole (lowering k from .15 to .14) shows:

$$DNPV = 50 - \frac{9.8}{1.14} + \frac{3.4}{1.14^2} + \frac{2.4}{1.14^3} + \frac{5.8}{1.14^4} + \frac{62.9}{1.14^5}$$

DNPV = $50 - $48.94 = $ 1.06 Million.

	1	2	3	4	5
Net Cash Inflow (NCF)	$ 9.80	$ 3.40	$ 2.40	$ 5.80	$ 62.90
PV of $1**	0.8772	0.7695	0.675	0.5921	0.5194
Present Value	$8.60	$2.62	$1.62	$3.43	$32.67
Total PV:	$48.94				

***Note: Table 1 = Present value interest factor for the cost of capital of 14%.

Using a lower discount rate lessened the DNPV by $1.68 million ($2.74 million - $1.06 million). This is reasonable in that the attractiveness of a divestment candidate at a certain selling price will be lessened as the candidate is found to be less risky.

Sensitivity Analysis

Sensitivity analysis is another technique that can be used in making divestiture decisions. In sensitivity analysis, the parent company evaluates the effect that certain factors have on the NCFs. For example, a divestment candidate's NCFs might be largely influenced by the price of copper, the US Navy Defense budget, and upcoming union contract talks. For these three influencing factors, a number of different scenarios or forecasts can be projected, each with their expected NCFs. For instance, the expected NCFs would be highest in the scenario where all three influencing factors are favorable. Having evaluated the NCFs and DNPVs for different scenarios, the parent firm has a better understanding of the range that the NCFs might fall in and also what factors influence them the most. Further, if the probability of the scenarios can be forecasted, statistical techniques can be used to give the probability of realizing a negative DNPV, the expected DNPV and the standard deviation, and coefficient of variation of DNPVs. This information would be very useful in making divestment decisions. It should be noted that the NCFs using sensitivity analysis are discounted at the firm's weighted average cost of capital.

Simulation

Simulation is a third technique used to account for the uncertainty of future cash flows. It is similar to but more sophisticated than the sensitivity analysis previously discussed. In simulation, the parent firm's managers first identify key factors that they believe are likely to influence the NCFs of a divestment candidate. Next they create a probability distribution describing the future outcome of each key factor. The managers finally must specify the impact of each key variable on the NCFs and ultimately the DNPVs. The firm's cost of capital is again used to discount the NCFs.

Computer programs are available to assist managers in the simulation analysis. After the data has been input and the program run, the computer will estimate NCFs and corresponding DNPVs over the whole range of probabilities. From this distribution, the analyst can determine the expected DNPV and the probability that the actual DNPV will be above or below some critical value. The uncertainty associated with the DNPV can also be determined, as measured by the dispersion of possible DNPV value. It is important to note that this technique is only as good as the input it receives from managers, and even then, it cannot make a firm's divestment decision. It does, however, provide a comprehensive evaluation of the divestiture proposal. *Note:* The major assumptions of the valuation must be clearly spelled out. A variety of "what-if" scenarios must be investigated to reduce valuation errors.

Closing the Form of the Transaction

Various considerations have an important impact on the form of the transaction.

Cash versus "Paper"

The seller's willingness to accept notes or stock of the buyer is determined partially by the personal need for current cash and more importantly by the quality and liquidity of the buyer's "paper." The seller who is not in need of immediate liquidity may, therefore, be somewhat flexible in this respect. The principal advantages of accepting the buyer's "paper" versus accepting cash are:

- ▶ It may increase the number of potential purchasers and the selling price.
- ▶ It may make it possible to structure the deal as a nontaxable transaction.
- ▶ If the interest and/or dividend rate is set at an attractively high level, it may present the seller with a better-yielding investment than he could otherwise obtain. The seller may be in a better position to follow and understand this investment as well.
- ▶ If attractively yielding preferred stock is taken back, the seller will hold a preferential position over common equity holders and the risk of a decline in value may, therefore, be lessened. Conversion, participation or other equity features may permit the seller to benefit from future appreciation of the underlying common stock.
- ▶ When marketable stock is received in a nontaxable transaction, the seller has substantial freedom in deciding when to "cash in" on his "realized" but

unrecognized gain. Future tax planning may be easier, and the shareholder may avoid bunching and alternative minimum tax problems.

▶ Installment sales reporting (matching the tax liability with collection of the principal on notes received) may allow for the deferral of tax payment to when the cash is received.

▶ Elderly stockholders may permanently escape the payment of tax by allowing the "paper" to be stepped-up to current fair value in their estate upon death.

Advantages of cash are:

▶ The risk of nonpayment does not exist.

▶ "Paper," particularly common stock, usually has considerable downside investment risk.

▶ The ability of successor management is not as important.

Installment Sales

Changes in the installment sales provisions have expanded their application to sales of businesses. The general purpose of these rules is to achieve a matching of the tax liability with the collection of cash. Thus, when one-tenth of the purchase price has been collected, one-tenth of the gain will be taxed. The principal changes are as follows:

▶ There is no longer a 30% limit on the amount that can be received in the year of the sale. Thus, the installment method can be utilized even when 90% of the sales price is collected in the year of the sale.

▶ Special rules have been added to make the installment method available when the purchase price is contingent in amount.

▶ Tax is no longer triggered when installment notes received during the course of a 12-month liquidation are distributed in the liquidation.

Contingent Earnout Arrangements

In both taxable and nontaxable transactions, the seller and the buyer may disagree on the growth potential for the business and, therefore, on its value. Such disagreements can be remedied by structuring an earnout contingency whereby the amount of stock issued or cash paid is increased if earnings exceed agreed levels. In nontaxable transactions, care must be exercised when incorporating such features. The IRS has published guidelines that can be followed to produce the desired results. In taxable transactions in which an allocation of the purchase price must be made, the rules regarding the allocation of contingent payments are unsettled. The IRS may assert that contingencies based upon future earnings should be treated as nondeductible goodwill.

Leveraged Buyouts (LBO)

The term "leveraged buyout" refers to a very popular form of taxable transaction in which the purchase price is funded primarily by lenders rather than by the buyer. *From the seller's perspective, it is a cash sale, but from the perspective of the purchaser, it is largely a "paper" transaction.* In a management leveraged buyout, key members of the management join or organize the buyer's equity group and must contribute their own funds or shares held in the seller's name to the transaction. These transactions are more complex than most because they involve additional participants (lenders, management and the equity investors), each of which must be satisfied with the transaction.

The tax consequences of the transaction are generally no different than those of any taxable transaction. Thus, the buyer must decide whether to take advantage of the step-up opportunities. Similarly, the sale of assets versus stock must also be analyzed by the participants.

Expanding Concept

The LBO is an evolving and expanding concept. The lenders are increasingly basing financing on cash flow rather than on the collateral value of assets, thereby making this a viable option for businesses with high cash flow but nominal physical assets. Because of the large profits that can be reaped by the equity participants, numerous leveraged buyout firms have been established, some of which specialize in smaller transactions. These firms have established relationships with interested lenders.

The LBO technique also permits the seller the choice of retaining a portion of his equity interest, thereby providing considerable flexibility to the seller in "cashing-out" versus sharing the future appreciation in the business' value.

What Makes a Good LBO Candidate?

The principal qualifications for a good LBO candidate are:
- Stable cash flow.
- Moderate growth prospects.
- Sound management.
- Ability to cover pro forma debt service and repay all debt in 10-20 years.

Regulated Investment Company Technique

If the selling shareholder(s) in a taxable transaction is not in need of cash but does have an interest in developing a diversified investment portfolio, an asset sale may be used advantageously. Instead of distributing the sales proceeds to the shareholder(s) and liquidating the corporation, which may result in substantial capital gains tax, the sale's proceeds could be left in the corporation and used to build the desired diversified investment portfolio. This technique is most popular when the tax basis of the corporation's assets is much greater than the shareholder's stock basis. In such a situation, a corporate sale of assets may produce a relatively low gain, or maybe even a loss, while the sale of the shareholder's stock may produce a much larger gain. In order to avoid or minimize the imposition of a duplicate tax on portfolio earnings, once to the corporation and a second time to the shareholder(s), this tactic requires either that the corporation invest in securities eligible for the 85% dividends-received deduction so that any double taxation is minimized, or that it qualify as a regulated investment company (more commonly known as a mutual fund), which means that there is at least 100 remaining stockholders. Regulated investment companies are not generally subject to corporate tax if they distribute the income earned to their shareholders. Of course, those stockholders who do desire cash may redeem their shares.

Recapitalizations

The "recapitalization" is a nontaxable exchange that is typically used to pass control of a corporation to new owners, frequently the younger generation. The recapitalization leaves the former owners with a nonappreciating but safer income-producing equity interest. Appreciation that accrues after the recapitalization is for the benefit of the new common stockholders.

This transaction does not provide current liquidity and generally does not require the involvement of investment bankers, except possibly to evaluate the worth of the business at the time of the recapitalization. This is a relatively old and well-established technique.

ESOP Techniques

ESOPs (*Employee Stock Ownership Plans*) are frequently used where broad-based employee ownership is appropriate. They are also used occasionally to provide more equity in a LBO. In these transactions the ESOP borrowings are used to purchase stock, thereby providing working capital to the employer corporation. The corporation makes an annual contribution to the plan to cover the ESOP's debt service. The contributions are fully tax deductible, even though they are comprised of interest and principal components.

Partial Sale Transactions

If the owner desires to maintain a substantial continuing equity position, he may wish to consider a transaction in which he sells only a portion of his interest in the business. The following transactions might accomplish this objective:
- Public offering of a minority position.
- Private placement of a minority position.
- Syndication of business real estate.

Accounting for Divestitures

The accounting method for divestitures in the financial statements of the divesting company depends on whether the unit being divested qualifies as "a segment of a business."

If a divestiture qualifies as a segment of a business, the results of operations of the divested entity should be retroactively deconsolidated and reported separately from income from continuing operations as a component of income before extraordinary items.

If the divestiture does not qualify as a segment of a business, the results of operations and assets and liabilities are still deconsolidated, but prospectively rather than retroactively. In addition, results of these operations cannot be reported separately as a discontinued business. Instead, they must be reported as part of income from continuing operations. If material, these results of operations should be disclosed separately as a component of income from continuing operations (e.g., as gain/loss on the sale of a business).

As per APB Opinion Number 29 (Accounting for Nonmonetary Transactions), a gain or loss cannot be recognized on a corporate divestiture. However, disclosure should be made of the nature and terms of the divestiture.

If there is an exchange of stock held by a parent in a subsidiary for stock of the parent company itself held by stockholders in the parent, there is a non-pro rata spinoff of the business segment because a reorganization is recorded at fair value. However, if there is a spinoff of a targeted company distributed on a pro rata basis to the one holding the applicable targeted stock, it should be recorded at historical cost as long as the targeted stock did not arise in contemplation of the later spinoff. If the contemplated situation did in fact exist, then the transaction is recorded at fair value. In a spinoff, there is a distribution of shares in the business segment, with the investor's shares being exchanged on a pro rata basis for the shares of the new company. In a spinoff, the transaction is, in effect, the purchase of treasury stock. Retained earnings is not changed.

In a spinoff, there is a distribution of the segment's shares to the investor's shareholders without the holders surrendering their shares.

In some cases, a spinoff may be treated as a discontinued operation of a business segment.

Example 28

J Company declares and pays a dividend to stockholders of 200,000 shares common stock of K Company. The investment in K Company at the date of spinoff under the equity method was $900,000.

The journal entries follow:

Retained earnings	900,000	
Property dividends payable		900,000
To record the declaration of the property dividend	.	
Property dividends payable	900,000	
Investment in V Company		900,000
To record the payment of the property dividend	.	

Note that in a spinoff no gain or loss is recorded.

Assume the same information except that in exchange for the 200,000 shares of K Company, J Company's stockholders give up 50,000 shares of J Company's common stock. The journal entry at the spinoff date is:

Treasury stock	900,000	
Investment in K Company		900,000

To reflect the purchase of treasury stock in exchange for the investment in K Company.

In a splitup, there is a transfer of the operations of the original entity to at least two *new* entities.

Example 29

L Company transfers Division A to M Company (a newly formed company) and its Division B to N Company (a newly formed company). L Company only had divisions A and B, so it terminates in existence. L Company shareholders receive a half share in M Company and a half share in N Company each one share of L Company.

Divisions A and B have the same book value of net assets.

Prior to the transfer, L Company's assets were $1,000,000, liabilities were $600,000, and equity was $400,000.

The liquidation entry to record the termination of L Company is:

Liabilities	600,000	
Stockholder's equity	400,000	
Assets		1,000,000

The entry to record M Company and N Company (the newly formed companies) would be identical based on the information given in this example. The entry is

Assets	500,000	
Liabilities		300,000
Paid-in-capital		200,000

Accounting for the Disposal of a Segment of a Business

APB Opinion No. 30 provides specific guidelines for accounting and reporting the effects of the disposal of a segment of a business. A "segment of a business" refers to a component of an entity whose activities represent a separate major line of business or class of customer. A segment may be in the form of a subsidiary, a division or a department, provided that its assets, results of operations and activities can be clearly distinguished — physically, operationally and for financial reporting purposes — from other assets, results of operations and activities of the entity. Operations of a segment that have been or will be sold or discontinued should be retroactively "deconsolidated" and reported separately from "income from continuing operations" on the face of the income statement as a "discontinued business" component of "income before extraordinary items?'

The assets and liabilities of the divestiture should also be deconsolidated and reported net in one or several summary lines in the balance sheet.

The actual or estimated gain or loss from disposal of a segment should be included in the reported results of operations of the segment in the year in which the divestiture plan is adopted.

Income from continuing operations before income taxes
Provision for income taxes
Income from continuing operations
Discontinued operations (Note 0):
Income (loss) from operations of discontinued Division X (less
applicable income taxes of $
Loss on disposal of Division X, including provision of $
operating losses during phaseout period (less applicable income
taxes of $
Net income

Dispositions in Form Only

Discontinued operations treatment should not be applied to the disposition of an operation when the risks of ownership have not, in substance, been transferred. This may be the case when (1) there is continuing involvement by the seller after disposal, (2) the principal consideration debt of the buyer with repayment depends on the success of future operations, or (3) significant debt or other performance guarantees are made by the seller. Although losses on such disposals should be recognized, gains should generally not be recognized until the uncertainty over the realization of the gain has been removed, at which time discontinued operations treatment should be applied.

Disclosure Requirements

APB Opinion No. 30 provides for significant disclosures relating to the disposal of a segment of a business. The disclosure requirements include the identity of the segment, expected disposal date, manner of disposal, a description of any remaining assets and liabilities of the segment at the balance-sheet date, income taxes applicable to the results of discontinued operations and the gain or loss and any proceeds expected from the disposal of the segment as of the balance-sheet date.

Expenses Related to a Divestiture

Under the provisions of *APB Opinion No. 30,* costs and expenses directly associated with the decision to dispose of a segment, which may include severance pay, additional pension costs, employee pension expenses and so on, must be charged to income as part of the results of operations of the discontinued business.

Subsidiaries Sold to the Public or Spun Off (Carveout Accounting)

When shares of a subsidiary (or a segment of a business that is subsequently incorporated) are initially sold to the public or spun off or when debt securities are initially sold to the public by a subsidiary, the SEC requires that the financial statements of the subsidiary in the prospectus include all expenses incurred by the parent on the subsidiary's behalf. To the extent that they have not been charged to the subsidiary in the past, the expenses must be retroactively reflected with the offsetting credit recorded in paid-in capital. The SEC's policy also applies to credits allocable to the subsidiary (e.g., management fees to the subsidiary in excess of the underlying cost of the services rendered). In such cases, the adjustment would be treated as a dividend to the parent.

The SEC also requires disclosure in the notes to the financial statements of management's estimates of what the expenses of the subsidiary would have been on a stand-alone basis when such expenses are significantly different from those reflected in the statements. Such estimates, however, should not be recorded in the historical statements. Further, it requires that the pro forma statements reflect or disclose (1) a separate-return income tax provision, (2) the effects of terminated or revised agreements with the parent, (3) dividends declared after the date of the balance sheet and (4) certain other adjustments. Lastly, in certain cases, historical earnings per share are not permitted and, when the entity was not a legal entity, retained earnings prior to incorporation may not be carried forward.

Liquidation Process

Divestment of a company or division is nearly always preferred to liquidation even though liquidation may provide the greatest potential for monetary gain. The reason why it is not the method of choice is that it usually takes longer to liquidate a business than it does to sell one outright. However, should the case exist where the value of the business is zero or less and no buyer can be found, liquidation becomes the obvious alternative. Liquidation may be so expensive that it is not feasible. Due to the cost of getting out of leases, contracts and possible salary continuation requirements, it may be cheaper to pay the existing management or entrepreneur to take over the business. The other option is bankruptcy.

The liquidation can be accomplished by contacting a liquidation company and having them perform all of the work involved in the liquidation process such as asset valuation, advertising the sale, negotiating the sale prices, and collecting the money for the goods. From this they will take a prenegotiated sum of money for their services. Another technique involves doing all the work in-house that the liquidation company would do and contacting competitors and various vendor representatives in the area and alert them to the fact you will be having a going out of business sale. They will typically already know you are about to go out of business since word has probably already spread in these circles.

Conclusion

The present business environment has made both divestiture and diversification an acceptable strategy for business to pursue. The requirement for public disclosure of business segment operating results has forced management to take action when a segment is not performing to company standards. Their action has been divestiture of the undesirable divisions. However, there are other alternatives for underperforming divisions. Divestiture has become an accepted method of dealing with problem business segments.

When developing the strategies involved with divestiture, management must consider the interrelationships between that division and the rest of the company and the costs of discontinuing that operation. The carrying out of a divestiture has an effect across the whole company including production, distribution, and marketing. Divestiture may also greatly affect the public's image of the company.

When considering divestiture as an alternative, all of these factors must be evaluated. The divestiture decision must be closely thought out.

Appendix

Present Value of $1

Periods	4%	6%	8%	10%	12%	14%	20%
1	0.962	0.943	0.926	0.909	0.893	0.877	0.833
2	0.925	0.890	0.857	0.826	0.797	0.769	0.694
3	0.889	0.840	0.794	0.751	0.712	0.675	0.579
4	0.855	0.792	0.735	0.683	0.636	0.592	0.482
5	0.822	0.747	0.681	0.621	0.567	0.519	0.402
6	0.790	0.705	0.630	0.564	0.507	0.456	0.335
7	0.760	0.665	0.583	0.513	0.452	0.400	0.279
8	0.731	0.627	0.540	0.467	0.404	0.351	0.233
9	0.703	0.592	0.500	0.424	0.361	0.308	0.194
10	0.676	0.558	0.463	0.386	0.322	0.270	0.162
11	0.650	0.527	0.429	0.350	0.287	0.237	0.135
12	0.625	0.497	0.397	0.319	0.257	0.208	0.112
13	0.601	0.469	0.368	0.290	0.229	0.182	0.093
14	0.577	0.442	0.340	0.263	0.205	0.160	0.078
15	0.555	0.417	0.315	0.239	0.183	0.140	0.065
16	0.534	0.394	0.292	0.218	0.163	0.123	0.054
17	0.513	0.371	0.270	0.198	0.146	0.108	0.045
18	0.494	0.350	0.250	0.180	0.130	0.095	0.038
19	0.475	0.331	0.232	0.164	0.116	0.083	0.031
20	0.456	0.312	0.215	0.149	0.104	0.073	0.026
30	0.308	0.174	0.099	0.057	0.033	0.020	0.004
40	0.208	0.097	0.046	0.022	0.011	0.005	0.001

Table 2: Present Value of an Annuity of $1

Periods	4%	6%	8%	10%	12%	14%	20%
1	0.962	0.943	0.926	0.909	0.893	0.877	0.833
2	1.886	1.833	1.783	1.736	1.690	1.647	1.528
3	2.775	2.673	2.577	2.487	2.402	2.322	2.106
4	3.630	3.465	3.312	3.170	3.037	2.914	2.589
5	4.452	4.212	3.993	3.791	3.605	3.433	2.991
6	5.242	4.917	4.623	4.355	4.111	3.889	3.326
7	6.002	5.582	5.206	4.868	4.564	4.288	3.605
8	6.733	6.210	5.747	5.335	4.968	4.639	3.837
9	7.435	6.802	6.247	5.759	5.328	4.946	4.031
10	8.111	7.360	6.710	6.145	5.650	5.216	4.192
11	8.760	7.887	7.139	6.495	5.938	5.453	4.327
12	9.385	8.384	7.536	6.814	6.194	5.660	4.439
13	9.986	8.853	7.904	7.103	6.424	5.842	4.533
14	10.563	9.295	8.244	7.367	6.628	6.002	4.611
15	11.118	9.712	8.559	7.606	6.811	6.142	4.675
16	11.652	10.106	8.851	7.824	6.974	6.265	4.730
17	12.168	10.477	9.122	8.022	7.120	6.373	4.775
18	12.659	10.828	9.372	8.201	7.250	6.467	4.812
19	13.134	11.158	9.604	8.365	7.366	6.550	4.844
20	13.590	11.470	9.818	8.514	7.469	6.623	4.870
30	17.292	13.765	11.258	9.427	8.055	7.003	4.979
40	19.793	15.046	11.925	9.779	8.244	7.105	4.997

Top 10 M&A Deals Worldwide

Top 10 M&A deals worldwide by value (in mil. USD) from 2000 to 2010:

Rank	Year	Purchaser	Purchased	Transaction value (in mil. USD)
1	2000	Fusion: AOL Inc. (America Online)	Time Warner	164,747
2	2000	Glaxo Wellcome Plc.	SmithKline Beecham Plc.	75,961
3	2004	Royal Dutch Petroleum Company	"Shell" Transport & Trading Co.	74,559
4	2006	AT&T Inc.	BellSouth Corporation	72,671
5	2001	Comcast Corporation	AT&T Broadband	72,041
6	2009	Pfizer Inc.	Wyeth	68,000
7	2000	Spin-off: Nortel Networks Corporation		59,974
8	2002	Pfizer Inc.	Pharmacia Corporation	59,515
9	2004	JPMorgan Chase & Co.	Bank One Corporation	58,761
10	2008	InBev Inc.	Anheuser-Busch Companies, Inc.	52,000

List of Bank Mergers in the United States

This is a partial list of many of the major banking company mergers since 1930 in the United States.

Year Merger closed	Acquirer	Acquired bank	Name of merged entity	Transaction Value	Ultimate Successor
1930	Chase National Bank	Equitable Trust Co. of NY	Chase National Bank		JPMorgan Chase & Co.
1930	Chase National Bank	Interstate Trust Co.	Chase National Bank		JPMorgan Chase & Co.
1948	Chemical Bank & Trust Co.	Continental Bank & Trust Co. of NY	Chemical Bank & Trust Co.		JPMorgan Chase & Co.
1951	Chemical Bank & Trust Co.	National Safety Bank & Trust Co. of NY	Chemical Bank & Trust Co.		JPMorgan Chase & Co.
1954	Chemical Bank & Trust Co.	Corn Exchange Bank & Trust Co.	Chemical Corn Exchange Bank		JPMorgan Chase & Co.
1955	National City Bank of New York	First National Bank of New York	First National City Bank		Citigroup
1955	Bank of the Manhattan Co.	Chase National Bank	Chase Manhattan Bank		JPMorgan Chase & Co.
1955	Bankers Trust	Public National Bank & Trust Co.	Bankers Trust		Deutsche Bank
1956	C&S of South Carolina	Growers Bank and Trust	C&S of South Carolina		Bank of America
1957	Commercial National Bank	American Trust Co.	American Commercial Bank		Bank of America
1957	Chase Manhattan Bank	Staten Island National Bank & Trust Co. of NY	Chase Manhattan Bank		JPMorgan Chase & Co.
1959	Chase Manhattan Bank	Clinton Trust Company	Chase Manhattan Bank		JPMorgan Chase & Co.
1959	Chemical Corn Exchange Bank	New York Trust Co.	Chemical Bank New York Trust Co.		JPMorgan Chase & Co.
1961	J. P. Morgan & Co.	Guaranty Trust Co. of NY	Morgan Guaranty Trust Co. of NY		JPMorgan Chase & Co.
1960	American Commercial Bank	Security National Bank	North Carolina National Bank		Bank of America
1961	Manufacturers Trust Co.	Hanover Bank	Manufacturers Hanover Bank		JPMorgan Chase & Co.

Year Merger closed	Acquirer	Acquired bank	Name of merged entity	Transaction Value	Ultimate Successor
1963	Chemical Bank New York Trust Co.	Bank of Rockville Centre Trust Co.	Chemical Bank New York Trust Co.		JPMorgan Chase & Co.
1964	Chemical Bank New York Trust Co.	First National Bank of Mount Vernon	Chemical Bank New York Trust Co.		JPMorgan Chase & Co.
1964	Chemical Bank New York Trust Co.	Bensonhurst National Bank of Brooklyn	Chemical Bank New York Trust Co.		JPMorgan Chase & Co.
1975	Chemical Bank	Security National Bank	Chemical Bank		JPMorgan Chase & Co.
1983	Mellon National Corp.	Girard Bank	Mellon National		Bank of New York Mellon
1983	BankAmerica Corp.	Seafirst Bank	BankAmerica Corp. (Seafirst banks operated as Seafirst until 1998)		Bank of America
1984	Chase Manhattan Corporation	Lincoln First Bank	Chase Manhattan Corporation (Chase Lincoln First until 1993)		JPMorgan Chase & Co.
1985	Bank of Boston Corp.	Colonial Bank	Bank of Boston Corp.		Bank of America
1985	Bank of Boston Corp.	Rhode Island Hospital Trust National Bank	Bank of Boston Corp.		Bank of America
1985	Bank of New England Corp.	The Connecticut Bank and Trust Co.	Bank of New England Corp.		Bank of America
1985	Citizens and Southern Georgia Corporation	Citizens and Southern National Bank of South Carolina	Citizens & Southern National Bank		Bank of America
1985	Trust Company of Georgia	SunBanks, Inc.	SunTrust Banks		SunTrust Banks
1985	Signet Banking Corporation	Union Trust Bancorp	Signet Banking Corporation		Wells Fargo
1986	Signet Banking Corporation	Security National Corp.	Signet Banking Corporation		Wells Fargo

Year Merger closed	Acquirer	Acquired bank	Name of merged entity	Transaction Value	Ultimate Successor
1986	Sovran Financial Corp.	Suburban Bank	Sovran Financial Corp.		Bank of America
1985	SunTrust Banks	Third National Corporation	SunTrust Banks		SunTrust Banks
1986	Security Pacific Corp.	The Arizona Bank	Security Pacific Corp.		Bank of America
1986	Wells Fargo Corp.	Crocker National Bank	Wells Fargo Corp. (combined California bank uses Crocker's charter)		Wells Fargo
1987	Chemical New York Corp.	Texas Commerce Bank	Chemical Banking Corporation (TX banks continued to operate as Texas Commerce)	$1.2 Billion	JPMorgan Chase & Co.
1987	The Fidelity Bank (Fidelcor)	First Fidelity Bank	First Fidelity Bank	$1.34 Billion- largest ever at the time	Wells Fargo
1987	RepublicBank Corp.	Interfirst Corp.	First Republic Bank Corp.		Bank of America
1987	Security Pacific Corp.	Rainier National Bank	Security Pacific Corp. (banks in Pacific NW continued to operate as Rainier)		Bank of America
1987	Sovran Financial Corp.	Commerce Union Bank	Sovran Financial Corp.		Bank of America
1987	U.S. Bancorp	Peoples National Bank of Washington	U.S. Bancorp		U.S. Bancorp
1987	Fleet Financial Group, Inc.	Norstar Bank	Fleet/Norstar Financial Group, Inc.		Bank of America
1987	First Union Corp.	Atlantic National Bank of Florida	First Union		Wells Fargo
1988	Bank of New York	Irving Trust Company	Bank of New York		Bank of New York Mellon

Year Merger closed	Acquirer	Acquired bank	Name of merged entity	Transaction Value	Ultimate Successor
1988	Shawmut Corp.	Hartford National Corp.	Shawmut National Corp.		Bank of America
1988	Shawmut Corp.	Arlington Trust Co.	Shawmut National Corp.		Bank of America
1988	First Bank System, Inc.	Central Bank of Denver	First Bank System, Inc. (Colo. banks never became First Bank due to name conflict)		U.S. Bancorp
1988	Wells Fargo Corp.	Barclays Bank of California, a subsidiary of Barclays plc	Wells Fargo Corp.		Wells Fargo
1988	Security Pacific Corp.	The Hibernia Bank	Security Pacific Corp.		Bank of America
1988	Credit Suisse	The First Boston Corporation	CS First Boston (later Credit Suisse First Boston)		Credit Suisse
1988	North Carolina National Bank	First Republic Bank Corporation	North Carolina National Bank		Bank of America
1989	Boatmen's Bancshares	Centerre Bank	Boatmen's Bancshares		Bank of America
1989	Security Pacific Corp.	Nevada National Bancorporation	Security Pacific Corp.		Bank of America
1989	Union Planter Bank	Magna Bank (Missouri)	Union Planters Bank		Regions Financial
1990	CoreStates Financial Corp.	First Pennsylvania Bank	CoreStates Financial Corp.		Wells Fargo
1990	First Union Corporation	Florida National Bank	First Union Corporation		Wells Fargo
1990	Citizens & Southern Bank	Sovran Financial Corp.	C&S/Sovran Corp.		Bank of America
1991	Fleet/Norstar Financial Group, Inc.	Bank of New England	Fleet/Norstar Financial Group, Inc.		Bank of America
1991	North Carolina National Bank	C&S/Sovran Corp.	NationsBank Corp.		Bank of America

Year Merger closed	Acquirer	Acquired bank	Name of merged entity	Transaction Value	Ultimate Successor
1991	Norwest Corp.	United Bank of Denver	Norwest Corp.		Wells Fargo
1991	Wachovia Corp.	The South Carolina National Bank	Wachovia Corp.		Wells Fargo
1991	First Union Corporation	Southeast Banking Corporation	First Union Corporation		Wells Fargo
1991	NBD Bancorp	Summcorp	NBD Bank	$323 million[1]	JPMorgan Chase & Co.
1991	Society Corp.	Ameritrust Corp.	Society Corp.		KeyBank
1991	Signet Banking Corporation	Madison National Bank	Signet Banking Corporation		Wells Fargo
1992	BankAmerica Corp.	Security Pacific	BankAmerica Corp.		Bank of America
1992	Keycorp	Puget Sound National Bank	Keycorp		KeyBank
1992	Barnett Banks, Inc.	First Florida Bank	Barnett Banks, Inc.		Bank of America
1992	Comerica, Inc.	Manufacturers Bank	Comerica		Comerica
1992	NBD Bancorp	INB Financial Corp.	NBD Bancorp	$876 million[2]	JPMorgan Chase & Co.
1992	Chemical Bank	Manufacturers Hanover Trust Company	Chemical Bank		JPMorgan Chase & Co.
1993	First Bank System, Inc.	Colorado National Bank	First Bank System, Inc. (CNB remained unchanged until after merger with U.S. Bancorp)		U.S. Bancorp
1993	Banc One Corp.	The Valley National Bank of Arizona	Banc One Corp.		JPMorgan Chase & Co.
1993	Bank of Boston Corp.	South Shore Bank, Mechanics Bank, First Agricultural	Bank of Boston Corp.		Bank of America
1993	First Union Corporation	Dominion Bank	First Union Corporation		Wells Fargo
1993	First Union Corporation	First American Bankcorp	First Union Corporation		Wells Fargo

Year Merger closed	Acquirer	Acquired bank	Name of merged entity	Transaction Value	Ultimate Successor
1993	NationsBank Corp.	Maryland National Bank	NationsBank Corp.		Bank of America
1993	NationsBank Corp.	American Security Bank	NationsBank Corp.		Bank of America
1994	Society Corp.	Keycorp	Keycorp		KeyBank
1994	Signet Banking Corporation	Pioneer Financial Corp.	Signet Banking Corporation		Wells Fargo
1994	BankAmerica Corp.	Continental Illinois National Bank	BankAmerica Corp.		Bank of America
1995	NBD Bancorp	Deerbank Corp.	NBD Bank	$120 million	JPMorgan Chase & Co.
1995	First Chicago Bank	NBD Bancorp	First Chicago NBD		JPMorgan Chase & Co.
1995	BB&T Corporation	Southern National Corp.	BB&T Corporation		BB&T
1995	Fleet Financial Group, Inc.	Shawmut National Corp.	Fleet Financial Group, Inc.		Bank of America
1996	Wells Fargo Corp.	First Interstate Bancorp	Wells Fargo Corp.		Wells Fargo
1996	Union Bank	Bank of California	Union Bank of California	$25 billion	Union Bank
1996	Chemical Banking Corp.	Chase Manhattan Corporation	Chase Manhattan Corporation		JPMorgan Chase & Co.
1996	CoreStates Financial Corp.	Meridian Bancorp, Inc.	CoreStates Financial Corp.		Wells Fargo
1996	Bank of Boston Corp.	BayBanks, Inc.	BankBoston Corp.		Bank of America
1996	First Union Corporation	First Fidelity Bancorporation	First Union Corporation		Wells Fargo
1996	First Union Corporation	Center Financial Corporation (CenterBank)	First Union Corporation		Wells Fargo
1996	Fleet Financial Group, Inc.	National Westminster Bancorp, a subsidiary of National Westminster Bank	Fleet Financial Group, Inc.		Bank of America
1996	Crestar Financial Corp.	Citizens Bancorp (Laurel, MD)	Crestar Financial Corp.		SunTrust Banks

123

Year Merger closed	Acquirer	Acquired bank	Name of merged entity	Transaction Value	Ultimate Successor
1997	U.S. Bancorp	First Bank System, Inc.	U.S. Bancorp		U.S. Bancorp
1997	NationsBank Corp.	Boatmen's Bancshares	NationsBank Corp.	$9.6 Billion	Bank of America
1997	Washington Mutual	Great Western Financial Corporation	Washington Mutual		JPMorgan Chase & Co.
1997	First Union Corporation	Signet Banking Corp.	First Union Corporation		Wells Fargo
1997	National City Corp.	First of America Bank	National City Corp.		PNC Financial Services
1997	Banc One Corp.	First USA	Bank One Corp.		JPMorgan Chase & Co.
1997	First Nationwide Bank	California Federal Bank	California Federal Bank	$1.2 billion ,1st Nationwide rebranded as "Cal Fed."	Citibank
1998	NationsBank Corp.	Barnett Banks, Inc.	NationsBank Corp.		Bank of America
1998	First Union Corporation	CoreStates Financial Corp.	First Union Corporation		Wells Fargo
1998	NationsBank Corp.	BankAmerica Corp.	Bank of America Corp.		Bank of America
1998	Golden State Bancorp	First Nationwide Holdings, Inc.	Golden State Bancorp	$5.8 billion	Citigroup
1998	Norwest Corp	Wells Fargo Corp.	Wells Fargo Corp.		Wells Fargo
1998	Star Banc Corp.	Firstar Holdings Corp.	Firstar Corporation		U.S. Bancorp
1998	Banc One Corp.	First Chicago NBD	Bank One Corp.		JPMorgan Chase & Co.
1998	Banc One Corp.	First Commerce Corp.	Bank One Corp.		JPMorgan Chase & Co.
1998	Travelers Group	Citicorp	Citigroup	$140 Billion	Citigroup
1998	SunTrust Bank	Crestar Financial Corp.	SunTrust Banks, Inc.		SunTrust Banks
1998	Washington Mutual	H.F. Ahmanson & Co.	Washington Mutual		JPMorgan Chase & Co.

Year Merger closed	Acquirer	Acquired bank	Name of merged entity	Transaction Value	Ultimate Successor
1999	Fleet Financial Corp.	BankBoston Corp.	FleetBoston Financial Corp.		Bank of America
1999	Deutsche Bank AG	Bankers Trust Corp.	Deutsche Bank AG		Deutsche Bank
1999	HSBC Holdings plc	Republic New York Corporation	HSBC Bank USA		HSBC Bank USA
1999	Firstar Corporation	Mercantile Bancorporation, Inc.	Firstar Corporation		U.S. Bancorp
1999	AmSouth Bancorporation	First American National Bank	AmSouth Bancorporation	$6.3 Billion	Regions Financial
2000	Chase Manhattan Corporation	J.P. Morgan & Co. Inc.	J.P. Morgan Chase & Co.		JPMorgan Chase & Co.
2000	Washington Mutual	Bank United Corp.	Washington Mutual	$1.5 Billion	JPMorgan Chase & Co.
2000	Wells Fargo & Co.	First Security Corp.	Wells Fargo & Co.		Wells Fargo
2000	UBS AG	Paine Webber	UBS AG		UBS AG
2001	Firstar Corporation	U.S. Bancorp	U.S. Bancorp		U.S. Bancorp
2001	First Union Corp.	Wachovia Corp.	Wachovia Corp.		Wells Fargo
2001	Fifth Third Bancorp	Old Kent Financial Corp.	Fifth Third Bancorp		Fifth Third Bank
2001	Standard Federal Bank	Michigan National Bank	Standard Federal Bank N.A.		Bank of America
2001	FleetBoston Financial Corp.	Summit Bancorp	FleetBoston Financial Corp.		Bank of America
2002	Citigroup Inc.	Golden State Bancorp	Citigroup Inc.	$5.8 billion	Citigroup
2002	Washington Mutual	Dime Bancorp, Inc.	Washington Mutual		JPMorgan Chase & Co.
2002	HSBC Holdings plc	Household International, Inc.	HSBC Bank USA		HSBC Bank USA
2003	BB&T Corp.	First Virginia Banks, Inc.	BB&T Corp.		BB&T
2003	M&T Bank	Allfirst Bank	M&T Bank		M&T Bank
2004	New Haven Savings Bank	Savings Bank of Manchester, Tolland Bank	NewAlliance Bank		NewAlliance Bank

Year Merger closed	Acquirer	Acquired bank	Name of merged entity	Transaction Value	Ultimate Successor
2004	North Fork Bancorporation Inc.	The Trust Company of New Jersey	North Fork Bancorporation Inc.	$726 Million	Capital One Financial
2004	Bank of America Corp.	FleetBoston Financial Corp.	Bank of America Corp.	$47 Billion	Bank of America
2004	J.P. Morgan Chase & Co.	Bank One	JPMorgan Chase & Co.		JPMorgan Chase & Co.
2004	Banco Popular	Quaker City Bank	Banco Popular		Banco Popular
2004	Regions Financial Corporation	Union Planters Corporation	Regions Financial Corporation	$5.9 Billion	Regions Financial
2004	SunTrust	National Commerce Financial	SunTrust	$6.98 Billion	SunTrust Banks
2004	Wachovia	SouthTrust	Wachovia	$14.3 Billion	Wells Fargo
2005	PNC Bank	Riggs Bank	PNC Bank	$0.78 billion	PNC Financial Services
2005	Capital One Financial Corporation	Hibernia National Bank	Capital One Financial Corporation	$4.9 Billion	Capital One Financial
2005	Bank of America	MBNA Corporation	Bank of America Card Services	$35 Billion	Bank of America
2006	Wachovia	Westcorp Inc. (holding company for WFS Financial Inc and Western Financial Bank)	Wachovia	$3.91 Billion	Wells Fargo
2006	NewAlliance Bank	Cornerstone Bank	NewAlliance Bank		NewAlliance Bank
2006	Capital One Financial Corporation	North Fork Bank	Capital One Financial Corporation	$13.2 Billion	Capital One Financial
2006	Wachovia	Golden West Financial	Wachovia	$25 Billion[8]	Wells Fargo
2006	Regions Financial Corporation	AmSouth Bancorporation	Regions Financial Corporation	$10 Billion	Regions Financial
2007	Citizens Banking Corporation	Republic Bancorp	Citizens Republic Bancorp	$1.048 Billion	Citizens Republic Bancorp

Year Merger closed	Acquirer	Acquired bank	Name of merged entity	Transaction Value	Ultimate Successor
2007	Banco Bilbao Vizcaya Argentaria USA	Compass Bancshares	BBVA Compass	$9.8 Billion	BBVA Compass
2007	Bank of America	LaSalle Bank	Bank of America	$21 Billion	Bank of America
2007	State Street Corporation	Investors Financial Services Corporation	State Street Corporation	$4.2 Billion	State Street Corporation
2007	Bank of New York	Mellon Financial Corporation	Bank of New York Mellon	$18.3 Billion	Bank of New York Mellon
2007	Wachovia	World Savings Bank	Wachovia	$25 Billion	Wells Fargo
2007	Bank of America	U.S. Trust Corporation	Bank of America Private Wealth Management		Bank of America
2007	M&T Bank	Partners Trust Financial Group	M&T Bank		M&T Bank
2008	TD Banknorth	Commerce Bancorp	TD Bank	$8.5 Billion	TD Bank
2008	JPMorgan Chase	Bear Stearns	JPMorgan Chase	$1.1 Billion	JPMorgan Chase & Co.
2008	Bank of America	Merrill Lynch	Bank of America	$50 Billion	Bank of America
2008	Wells Fargo	Wachovia	Wells Fargo	$15.1 Billion	Wells Fargo
2008	JPMorgan Chase	Washington Mutual	JPMorgan Chase	$1.9 Billion	JPMorgan Chase & Co.
2008	Fifth Third Bank	First Charter Bank	Fifth Third Bank	$1.1 billion	Fifth Third Bank
2008	PNC Financial Services	National City Corp.	PNC Financial Services	$5.08 billion	PNC Financial Services
2008	U.S. Bancorp	Downey Savings and Loan	U.S. Bancorp		U.S. Bancorp
2009	M&T Bank	Provident Bank of Maryland	M&T Bank		M&T Bank
2009	M&T Bank	Bradford Bank	M&T Bank		M&T Bank
2011	M&T Bank	Wilmington Trust	M&T Bank		M&T Bank
2011	Capital One	ING Direct USA	Capital One	$9 billion	Capital One

Letter of Intent to Purchase – Non Binding – Asset Purchase

NAME

BUSINESS NAME ADDRESS DATE

Re: Letter of Intent to Purchase – Non Binding – Asset Purchase

Dear NAME:

This letter agreement sets forth our agreement and understanding as to the essential terms of the sale to PURCHASER (the "Purchaser") by SELLER (the "Seller") of the Seller's BUSINESS (the "Business"), located in ADDRESS and engaged in BUSINESS DESCRIPTION. The parties intend this letter agreement to be non-binding and unenforceable until which time the terms are agreed upon. Subsequently, The Binding Letter of Intent to Purchase will inure to the benefit of the parties and their respective successors and assigns.

Asset Purchase. At the closing, the Purchaser will purchase substantially all of the assets associated with the Business, including all inventories, all intellectual property, all accounts and notes receivable, most contracts and agreements, all equipment, all legally assignable government permits, and certain documents, files and records containing technical support and other information pertaining to the operation of the Business.

1. Excluded Assets include EXCLUDED ASSETS, all written and verbal contracts not disclosed in writing during due diligence, others may arise during the course of Due Diligence.
2. Liabilities
   a.) Assumed Liabilities. The Purchaser will assume as of the closing date only those liabilities and obligations
      (i) arising in connection with the operation of the Business by the Purchaser after the closing date, and
      (ii) arising after the closing date in connection with the performance by the Purchaser of the contracts and agreements associated with the Business.
   b.) Excluded Liabilities include EXCLUDED LIABILITIES, any verbal or written contracts not disclosed in writing to the Sellers during Due Diligence, others may arise during the course of Due Diligence.
3. Purchase Price. The purchase price will be DESCRIBE PURCHASE PRICE (in broad terms including the total transaction value, cash down payment, and any Seller Note) payable in cash in immediately available funds on the closing date.

4. Pre-Closing Covenants. The parties will use their reasonable best efforts to obtain all necessary third-party and government consents (including all certificates, permits and approvals required in connection with the Purchaser's operation of the Business). The Seller will continue to operate the Business consistent with past practice. Accounts Receivable and Accounts Payable will be managed status quo and will not accelerate or decelerate in days outstanding. The parties agree to prepare, negotiate and execute a purchase agreement which will reflect the terms set forth in this letter agreement, and will contain customary representations and warranties.

5. Conditions to Obligation. The Purchaser and the Seller will be obligated to consummate the acquisition of the Business unless the Purchaser has failed to obtain, despite the parties' reasonable best efforts, all certificates, permits and approvals that are required in connection with Purchaser's operation of the Business.

6. Due Diligence. The Seller agrees to cooperate with the Purchaser's due diligence investigation of the Business and to provide the Purchaser and its representatives with prompt and reasonable access to key employees and to books, records, contracts and other information pertaining to the Business (the "Due Diligence Information").

7. Confidentiality; Non-competition. The Purchaser will use the Due Diligence Information solely for the purpose of the Purchaser's due diligence investigation of the Business, and unless and until the parties consummate the acquisition of the Business the Purchaser, its affiliates, directors, officers, employees, advisors, and agents (the Purchaser's "Representatives") will keep the Due Diligence Information strictly confidential. The Purchaser will disclose the Due Diligence Information only to those Representatives of the Purchaser who need to know such information for the purpose of consummating the acquisition of the Business. The Purchaser agrees to be responsible for any breach of this paragraph 7 by any of the Purchaser's Representatives. In the event the acquisition of the Business is not consummated, the Purchaser will return to the Seller any materials containing Due Diligence Information, or will certify in writing that all such materials or copies of such materials have been destroyed. The Purchaser also will not use any Due Diligence Information to compete with the Seller in the event that the acquisition of the Business is not consummated. The provisions of this paragraph 7 will survive the termination of this letter agreement. Buyers expect that no employee, owner or stakeholder will take customers with them to competing businesses during due diligence or after closing.

8. Employees of the Business. Until the consummation of the acquisition of the Business, or in the event that the parties do not consummate the acquisition of the Business, the Purchaser will not solicit or recruit the employees of the Business.

9. Exclusive Dealing. Until December 31, 2010, the Seller will not enter into any agreement, discussion, or negotiation with, or provide information to, or solicit, encourage, entertain or consider any inquiries or proposals from, any other corporation, fire or other person with respect to (a) the possible disposition of a material portion of the Business, or (b) any business combination involving the Business, whether by way of merger, consolidation, share exchange or other transaction. If for any reason the acquisition of the Business is not consummated, and the Seller is unable to enforce the provisions of this letter agreement, the Buyer will pay to the Seller a break-up fee which will equal the sum of 1% of the purchase price, and the Seller's expenses in connection with the negotiation of the acquisition.

10. Public Announcement. All press releases and public announcements relating to the acquisition of the Business will be agreed to and prepared jointly by the Seller and the Purchaser.

11. Expenses. Subject to the provisions in paragraph 9 of this letter agreement, each party will pay all of its expenses, including legal fees, incurred in connection with the acquisition of the Business.

12. Indemnification: The Seller represents and warrants that the Purchaser will not incur any liability in connection with the consummation of the acquisition of the Business to any third party with whom the Seller or its agents have had discussions regarding the disposition of the Business, and the Seller agrees to indemnify, defend and hold harmless the Purchaser, its officers, directors, stockholders, lenders and affiliates from any claims by or liabilities to such third parties, including any legal or other expenses incurred in connection with the defense of such claims. The covenants contained in this paragraph 12 will survive the termination of this letter agreement.

If you are in agreement with the terms of this letter agreement, please sign in the space provided below and return a signed copy to NAME, BUSINESS NAME, and ADRESS by the close of business on DATE. Upon receipt of a signed copy of this letter, we will proceed with our plans for consummating the transaction in a timely manner.

Very truly yours, PURCHASER

By:

NAME, TITLE

SELLER

By:

NAME, TITLE

Mutual Confidentiality Agreement

This Mutual Confidentiality Agreement ("Agreement") is entered into as of the <u>DATE</u> (the "Effective Date"), by and between <u>COMPANY A.,</u> with a main address <u>ADDRESS,</u> (hereafter "Company A") and <u>COMPANY B</u> with an address at <u>ADDRESS</u>

1) The parties acknowledge and agree that it may be necessary or desirable for one or both parties to disclose to the other party certain proprietary or otherwise confidential information ("Confidential Information") regarding a proposed business relationship between the parties.

2) The parties agree that all Confidential Information which is disclosed by either party to the other party during the term of this Agreement shall be maintained in secrecy by the receiving party during the term of this Agreement and for a period of two (2) years thereafter using the same safeguards as the receiving party uses to protect its own commercially confidential information of a similar character, but at least using reasonable care.

3) The parties agree that the receiving party shall not disclose any Confidential Information to any third party and shall not use any Confidential Information for any purpose other than the evaluation of the proposed or ongoing business relationship contemplated herein.

4) The parties acknowledge and agree that Confidential Information shall not include any information which is or becomes:

   a. Already known to or otherwise in the possession of the receiving party at the time of receipt from the disclosing party;

   b. Publicly available or otherwise in the public domain;

   c. Rightfully obtained by the receiving party from any third party without restriction and without breach of this Agreement by the receiving party;

   d. Released by the disclosing party to any third party without restrictions or

   e. Disclosed without restriction pursuant to judicial action or governmental regulations or other requirements by the receiving party provided the receiving party has notified the disclosing party prior to such disclosure and cooperates with the disclosing party in the event the disclosing party elects to legally contest and avoid such disclosure.

5) The parties acknowledge that Confidential Information does not include any information which is hereafter developed independently by a person or persons who have not had either direct or indirect contact with the relevant information furnished by the disclosing party

6) No formal business organization or relationship of any kind is established or intended to be established by this Agreement.

7) This Agreement shall be subject to and construed in accordance with the laws of the State of STATE.

8) This Agreement shall inure to the benefit of and be binding upon all parties hereto and to their respective successors and legal representatives.

9) No provision of this Agreement will be waived by any party except in writing. The parties hereto agree that the waiver by any party of a breach of any provision of this Agreement shall not operate or be construed as a waiver of any subsequent breach of that provision by the same party, or any other provision or condition of this Agreement.

10) If any provision or application of this Agreement shall be held invalid or unenforceable, the remaining provisions and applications of this Agreement shall not be affected, but rather shall remain valid and enforceable.

11) This Agreement constitutes the entire agreement and supersedes any and all other understandings and agreements between the parties with respect to the subject matter hereof and no representation, statement, or promise not contained herein shall be binding on either party. This Agreement may be modified only by a written amendment duly signed by persons authorized to sign agreements on behalf of the parties and shall not be supplemented or modified by any course of dealing or trade usage.

COMPANY A   COMPANY B

By: By:

Title: Title:

Date: Date:

Due Diligence Checklist

Section I. Organization & Corporate Records			
Item	**Description**	**Comment**	**Received?**
I.1 Initial Organization	Documents related to organization of the company prior to incorporation.		
I.2 Organizational Changes	Documents related to acquisitions, restructurings, reorganizations, bankruptcies, dispositions, repurchases, and changes of form (e.g. from a partnership to an LLC)		
I.3 Articles	Articles of incorporation and all amendments thereto		
I.4 Bylaws	Corporate bylaws and all amendments thereto		
I.5 Minutes	Minutes of the board of directors, including shareholder resolutions, written consents, and the minutes of any director or executive committees		
I.6 Shareholder Communications	All communications with shareholders including annual reports, letters, solicitations and proxy statements		
I.7 Stock Ledger	The stock ledger for the Company and each subsidiary.		
I.8 Share Records	A list of all shares authorized, issued and outstanding.		
I.9 Securities Agreements	Agreements relating to options, option plans, voting trusts, warrants, agreements to issues securities, calls, agreements to purchase securities, puts, subscriptions, ESPPs, stock bonus plans, and convertible securities.		

I.10 Equity Compensation	All equity compensation agreements, including a list of all participants, the number of shares they own, the restrictions on those shares, and their exercise price.		
I.11 Shareholder Agreements	All agreements with shareholders relating to voting, acquisition, redemption or disposition of securities.		
I.12 Change of Control Plans	All documents relating to anti-takeover measures or any agreement, plan or document that contains change of control provisions.		
I.13 Org Charts	Organization charts showing ownership and operational structure, including information related to subsidiaries, divisions, joint ventures and affiliates.		
I.14 Certificates	Certificate of Good Standing from the secretary of state of incorporation, as well as any other		
I.15 List of Jurisdictions	List of all states, provinces, or countries where the Company owns or leases property, maintains employees, or is otherwise authorized to do business.		
Section II. Financial Information			
Item	**Description**	**Comment**	**Received?**
II.1 Financial Statements	All annual and quarterly financial statements for the past 5 years for the Company and all its subsidiaries.		
II.2 Interim Financial Statements	The latest available interim financial information (e.g. unaudited monthly financial statements).		
II.3 Auditor Communications	All communications with auditors, including auditors letters and replies, PBC lists, and other correspondence for the past 5 years.		

II.4 Budgets	All available company-wide and departmental budgets for the last 5 years		
II.5 Projections	The latest financial projections and estimates for the Company and its subsidiaries, including a discussion of assumptions made.		
II.6 Capital budgets	The latest available capital budget, including a discussion of essential, non-essential and strategic investments		
II.7 Cash	A detailed schedule of all cash holdings and short-term investments		
II.8 Inventory	A detailed schedule of inventory by product and geography		
II.9 Accounts Receivable	A detailed aged schedule of accounts receivable by customer and geography		
II.10 Long term investments	A detailed schedule of long term investments, including share holding, bonds and debt instruments		
II.11 Property, Plant & Equipment	A detailed schedule of all property, plant and equipment, including acquisition cost, accumulated depreciation, and depreciable life		
II.12 Accounts payable	A detailed schedule of all accounts payable by vendor		
II.13 Debt	A detailed schedule of all outstanding notes payable, bonds, mortgages and other long term debts		
II.14 Orders booked	A detailed schedule by customer of orders booked for the past 5 years		
II.15 Revenues and cost of sales	A detailed schedule of revenues and cost of sales broken down by customer, geography, and product for the past 5 years		

II.16 SG&A	A detailed schedule of selling, general and administrative expenses by division, subsidiary and geography for the past 5 years		
II.17 Contingent liabilities	A detailed schedule of all contingent liabilities		
II.18 Off-balance sheet items	A detailed schedule of all off-balance sheet transactions including lease liabilities and credit derivatives		
II.19 Capital expenditures	A detailed schedule of all capital expenditures for the past 5 years, including a description of each major expenditure		
II.20 Restructurings	A detailed schedule of any restructurings, reorganizations or major operational changes undertaken in the past 5 years		
II.21 Accounting changes	A schedule of any changes in accounting policies, principles or procedures in the past 5 years, including an explanation of why such changes were made		
II.22 Controls	A detailed description of the Company's internal controls		
II.23 Reserves	Details of any reserves held (e.g. reserve for obsolete inventory)		
II.24 Intercompany transactions	Details of all transactions between the company and its subsidiaries, parents, or other related parties.		
II.25 Extraordinary items	Details and descriptions of any extraordinary or non-recurring items appearing in the financial statements during the past 5 years		
II.26 Deferred income	A detailed schedule of all deferred income items for the past 5 years		
II.27 Accounting policies	A detailed description of all accounting policies, including depreciation methods		

Item	Description	Comment	Received?
II.28 Breakeven cash flow analysis	An analysis of the company's monthly breakeven cash flow, broken down by fixed and variable cash inflows and outflows		
II.29 Financial services	Description of services provided by accountants, auditors, financial advisors, actuaries, brokers and other financial professionals for the past 5 years		
Section III. Legal, Regulatory & Compliance			
Item	**Description**	**Comment**	**Received?**
III.1 Litigation	A detailed schedule of all ongoing, pending and threatened action, arbitration, audit, examination, investigation, hearing, litigation, claim, suit, administrative proceeding, governmental investigation, or governmental inquiry affecting the Company, its assets or operations		
III.2 Regulators correspondence	Copies of all correspondence, reports to and filings with all regulators, including but not limited to the Securities & Exchange Commission, state securities authorities, foreign securities authorities, the Department of Justice, the Environmental Protection Agency, and the Department of Commerce.		
III.3 Court orders	A detailed schedule of all court orders, writs, judgments, injunctions, decrees and settlements to which the Company is a party		

III.4 Notices	Copies of all notices of legal or regulatory violations and infringements including correspondence, reports, notices, and filings related to any dispute, alleged violation or infringement by the Company, its agents or employees of any local, state, federal or foreign lawn, regulation, order or permit relating to employment violations, unfair labor practices, equal opportunity, bribery, corruption, occupational safety and health, antitrust matters, intellectual property and environmental matters.		
III.5 Permits	All local, state, federal and foreign approvals, authorizations, certifications, clearances, licenses, permits, registrations and waivers related to the Company, its operations or assets		
III.6 Breaches and defaults	A detailed schedule of all breaches or defaults that have occurred under agreements to which the Company is a party, including all agreements which would be affected by the contemplated transaction (e.g. change of control provisions).		
Section IV. Taxes			
Item	**Description**	**Comment**	**Received?**
IV.1 Returns	All local, state, federal and foreign tax returns and filings (including sales tax returns) made by the Company for the past 5 years		

IV.2 Tax authority correspondence	All correspondence with local, state, federal and foreign tax authorities including audits, revenue agents' reports and notices of proposed or final adjustments to the Company's tax liabilities for the past 5 years		
IV.3 Determination Letters	Any determination letters from the IRS or other tax authority received in the past 5 years		
IV.4 Settlements	All agreements, consents, elections, requests, rulings, settlements and waivers made with any local, state, federal or foreign tax authority in the past 5 years		
IV.5 Compliance	All documents related to the Company's compliance with tax laws and regulations for the past 5 years		
IV.6 Opinions	All tax opinions received from attorneys, accountants or other specialists for the past 5 years		
IV.7 Open years	A detailed schedule of all open years for local, state, federal and foreign taxes		
IV.8 Jurisdictions	A detailed schedule of all tax jurisdictions (including sales tax jurisdictions) where the Company operates, maintains a physical presence of any kind or has employees or agents		
IV.9 Tax liabilities	A detailed schedule of all tax liabilities		
IV.10 Tax basis	A detailed schedule of the tax basis of all assets, its accumulated depreciation and the depreciation method used		

IV.11 Carryforwards and carrybacks	A detailed schedule of all tax carryforwards and carrybacks, including their source (e.g. net operating loss or foreign tax credit), their expiration dates and any limitations on their use		
IV.12 Tax free transactions	A detailed schedule of all tax free transactions not listed on the Company's tax returns		
IV.13 Transfer pricing	A description of transfer pricing methodologies		
IV.14 Tax liens	A detailed schedule of all tax liens against the Company's assets		
Section V. Intellectual Property			
Item	**Description**	**Comment**	**Received?**
V.1 IP portfolio	A detailed schedule of all patents, patent applications, trademarks, trademark applications, trade names, trade name applications, copyrights, copyright applications, service marks and service mark applications owned, held or used by the Company, including ownership, adverse claims made, involvement in litigation (if any), jurisdiction of registration and registration status.		
V.2 Trade secrets	A description of trade secrets and other unpatented proprietary information		
V.3 Know how	A description of significant technical know-how used by the Company		
V.4 License agreements	A detailed schedule of all license agreements to which the Company is a party		
V.5 Royalty agreements	A detailed schedule of all royalty agreements to which the Company is a party		

V.6 Technology sharing	A detailed schedule of all technology sharing agreements to which the Company is a party		
V.7 Other IP agreements	A detailed schedule of all agreements related to intellectual property, including use of technology or information, disclosure of information and confidentiality.		
V.8 Domain names	A schedule of all internet websites and domain names owned or used by the Company		
V.9 Software	A detailed schedule of all software assets owned or licensed by the Company		
V.10 Infringement	A detailed schedule of all potential or current matters relating to infringement, interference, or unfair competition		

Section VI. Employee Matters

Item	Description	Comment	Received?
VI.1 Officers and directors	A list of all officers and directors of the Company.		
VI.2 Org charts	Organizational charts describing the Company's management structure and lines of reporting.		
VI.3 Key employees	A list of all key employees, their function, their salary, their resume and their importance to the business.		
VI.4 Employee list	A list of all employees including position, salary, and location.		
VI.5 Consultants and contractors	A list of all consultants and contractors working for the Company.		
VI.6 Employment agreements	All employment, consulting, change-of-control, non-disclosure, non-solicitation , or non-competition agreements between the Company and any of its employees, contractors or consultants.		

VI.7 Bonus plans	Documents describing any bonus, incentive or profit-sharing plans including funding requirements and schedules of amounts paid under the plan for the past 5 years.		
VI.8 Pension plans	Documents describing any retirement or pension plans including funding requirements; actuarial reports; financial reports or financial summaries; IRS Form 5500, 5310, or 5330; annual reports, reportable event notices, notices of intent to terminate a plan filed with the Pension Benefit Guarantee Corporation; any applications for determination filed with the IRS; and schedules of amounts paid under the plan for the past 5 years.		
VI.9 Insurance plans	Documents describing any group life insurance, death benefit, disability, accident, cafeteria, health, major medical, medical expense reimbursement, dependent care or sick leave policies or programs, including funding requirements; actuarial reports; financial reports or financial summaries; IRS Form 5500, 5310, or 5330; annual reports, reportable event notices, notices of intent to terminate a plan filed with the Pension Benefit Guarantee Corporation; any applications for determination filed with the IRS; and schedules of amounts paid under the plan for the past 5 years.		

VI.10 Vacation plans	Documents describing any holiday, vacation, leave-of-absence or sabbatical plans, including funding requirements; actuarial reports; financial reports or financial summaries; IRS Form 5500, 5310, or 5330; annual reports, reportable event notices, notices of intent to terminate a plan filed with the Pension Benefit Guarantee Corporation; any applications for determination filed with the IRS; and schedules of amounts paid under the plan for the past 5 years.		
VI.11 Stock plans	Documents describing any stock option, stock purchase, stock appreciation right, stock bonus, employee stock option and employee stock ownership plans, including funding requirements; actuarial reports; financial reports or financial summaries; IRS Form 5500, 5310, or 5330; annual reports, reportable event notices, notices of intent to terminate a plan filed with the Pension Benefit Guarantee Corporation; any applications for determination filed with the IRS; and schedules of amounts paid under the plan for the past 5 years.		

VI.12 Savings plans and other employee benefit plans	Documents describing any savings, deferred compensation, supplemental unemployment benefit, welfare, salary continuation, severance pay, termination pay, change-in-control, worker's compensation or other employee benefit plan, including funding requirements; actuarial reports; financial reports or financial summaries; IRS Form 5500, 5310, or 5330; annual reports, reportable event notices, notices of intent to terminate a plan filed with the Pension Benefit Guarantee Corporation; any applications for determination filed with the IRS; and schedules of amounts paid under the plan for the past 5 years.		
VI.13 ERISA Plans	Documents describing any plan that qualifies as an "employee pension benefit plan" or "employee welfare benefit plan" as defined by Section 3 of the Employee Retirement Income Security Act of 1974.		
VI.14 Collective bargaining agreements	Copies of any collective bargaining agreements related to any labor unions or other employee groups.		
VI.15 Reductions in force	Details of any reductions-in-force made by the Company within the past 12 months, including lists of employees made redundant and the costs of such reductions-in-force.		
VI.16 Employee disputes	A detailed schedule of any allegations of wrongful termination, harassment, discrimination or other employee disputes for the past 5 years.		

VI.17 Litigation	A detailed schedule of all employee or labor related litigation and investigations, whether settled, ongoing, or pending, over the past 5 years.		
VI.18 Labor relations disputes	A detailed schedule of any labor disputes, requests for arbitration, or grievances filed or pending within the past 5 years.		
VI.19 Code of ethics	Copies of codes of ethics or conduct used by the Company.		
Section VII. Contracts			
Item	**Description**	**Comment**	**Received?**
VII.1 Contracts with other organizations	A detailed schedule of all subsidiaries, partnerships, joint ventures and strategic alliances along with copies of all related agreements.		
VII.2 Contracts with related parties	Copies of all contracts between the Company and its officers, directors, shareholders and affiliates.		
VII.3 Contracts with creditors	Copies of all loan agreements, bank financing agreements, lines of credit, promissory notes, security agreements, mortgages, indentures, collateral pledges or other contracts with creditors.		
VII.4 Guaranties and indemnity agreements	Copies of all agreements that obligate the Company to indemnify a third party, or that otherwise commits the Company to provide a guarantee of any kind.		
VII.5 Sales agreements	Copies of all contracts related to sales, agency, franchise, dealer, marketing or distribution agreements or arrangements.		
VII.6 Supply agreements	Copies of all contracts related to supplier or vendor agreements.		
VII.7 Customer contracts	Copies of all customer agreements with a value of $_____ or greater.		

VII.8 Licensing, franchise and conditional sales	Copies of all licensing agreements, franchise agreements and conditional sales agreements to which the Company is party.		
VII.9 Quotes	Copies of all outstanding bids, quotations or tenders with a potential value of $____ or greater.		
VII.10 Purchase orders	Copies of the Company's standard quote, purchase order and invoice forms, including standard terms and conditions.		
VII.11 M&A	Copies of any memoranda of understanding, letters of intent, contracts, agreements, or closing documents related to any acquisition or disposition of corporate shares, companies, divisions, businesses, or other significant assets by the Company.		
VII.12 Noncompetition agreements	Copies of any agreements that prohibit, limit or restrain the Company from engaging in any business activity or otherwise competing with another entity.		
VII.13 Nondisclosure agreements	Copies of any nondisclosure agreements to which the Company is a party.		
VII.14 Other material agreements	Copies of all agreements with a value of $____ or greater, or which have a material impact on the operation of the business, and are not requested elsewhere in this checklist.		
Section VIII. Real & Personal Property			
Item	**Description**	**Comment**	**Received?**
VIII.1 Business locations	A detailed schedule of all locations where Company business is transacted, including offices, warehouses, stores and factories.		

VIII.2 Owned real estate	A detailed schedule of all real estate owned by the Company.		
VIII.3 Titles and rights to owned real estate	A copy of the deed or title to any real estate owned by the Company as well as a description of all rights attached to the property (e.g. air or mineral rights)		
VIII.4 Debts and encumbrances on owned real estate	A detailed schedule of all debts, liens or other encumbrances on real estate owned by the Company.		
VIII.5 Other documents related to owned real estate	A copy of all surveys, zoning approvals, variances, use permits or appraisals related to real estate owned by the Company.		
VIII.6 Leased real estate	A detailed schedule of all real estate rented or leased by the Company. This schedule should contain a brief description of the lease terms, including amount and frequency of rent and the remaining term of the lease or rent agreement.		
VIII.7 Owned personal property	A detailed schedule of all personal property owned by the Company with a value of $_____ or greater. This schedule should include a description of the property, its location, its book value, and any debt or encumbrances on the property. This schedule should include all inventories, machinery and equipment, tools, furniture, office equipment, computer hardware and software, supplies, materials, vehicles and fixtures.		

Item	Description	Comment	Received?
VIII.8 Leased personal property	A detailed schedule of all personal property rented or leased by the Company with a value of $_____ or greater. This schedule should include a description of the property, its location, its book value, the amount and frequency of rent and the remaining term of the lease or rent agreement. This schedule should include all inventories, machinery and equipment, tools, furniture, office equipment, computer hardware and software, supplies, materials, vehicles and fixtures.		
VIII.9 Lien search	The results of any lien searches.		
VIII.10 UCC filings	A schedule of all UCC filings on the assets of the Company.		
VIII.11 Capital equipment purchases and disposals	A detailed schedule of all capital equipment purchases and dispositions made during the past 5 years.		

Section IX. Credit Facilities

Item	Description	Comment	Received?
IX.1 Long-term debt facilities	A detailed schedule of all long-term debt facilities, including capitalized leases, guarantees and other contingent obligations, along with copies of all related documents.		
IX.2 Short-term debt facilities	A detailed schedule of all short-term debt facilities, including capitalized leases, guarantees and other contingent obligations, along with copies of all related documents.		
IX.3 Correspondence	Copies of all correspondence with lenders including consents, notices, waivers of default, and compliance certificates.		

Section X. Environmental Matters

Item	Description	Comment	Received?
X.1 Permits	A detailed schedule of all permits, licenses, registrations, notices, approvals, certifications, contingency plans and any other authorization related to environmental, health or safety matters.		
X.2 Audits	Environmental audits for each property owned or leased by the Company.		
X.3 Hazardous materials	A detailed schedule of all hazardous substances (including dangerous, toxic, radioactive, or infectious substances, materials, pollutants, contaminants or waste) that the Company has or may have used, stored, generated, treated, handled, released or disposed of.		
X.4 Disposal methods	A description of the Company's methods of handling, treating, storing, securing, transporting, recycling, reclaiming and disposing of hazardous materials. This should include a detailed schedule describing all wells, above-ground storage tanks, below-ground storage tanks, surface impoundments, and any other waste disposal facility owned, operated or used by the Company to store or dispose of hazardous materials.		

X.5 Internal reports	Copies of all internal reports (whether created by Company personnel or a 3rd Party) relating to environmental, health or safety matters. Such reports should include emissions monitoring results, sample testing results, laboratory analyses, and monitoring logs.		
X.6 Regulators	Copies of all statements, reports and correspondence involving the Environmental Protection Agency or any other environmental, health or safety regulatory group, agency or body.		
X.7 Environmental, health or safety related litigation	A detailed schedule of all environmental, health or safety related litigation and investigations, whether settled, ongoing, or pending, over the past 5 years.		
Section XI. Related Parties			
Item	**Description**	**Comment**	**Received?**
XI.1 Contracts	Copies of any contracts or agreements between the Company and any current or former director, officer, shareholder or affiliate of the Company.		
XI.2 Receivables and payables	A detailed schedule of any amounts owed by the Company to any current or former director, officer, shareholder or affiliate of the Company and any amount owed by any current or former director, officer, shareholder or affiliate of the Company to the Company.		
XI.3 Other transactions	Copies of documents relating to any other transaction between the Company and any current or former director, officer, shareholder or affiliate of the Company.		

XI.4 Conflicts of interest	Describe any interests of any current or former director, officer, shareholder or affiliate of the Company in any business that competes with, conducts any business similar to, or has any arrangement or agreement with the Company.		

Section XII. Securities & Investments

Item	Description	Comment	Received?
XII.1 Equity investments	A detailed schedule of companies in which the Company holds an interest of 5% or more.		
XII.2 Offering documents	Copies of all offering circulars, private placement memoranda, syndication documents, or other securities placement documents, prepared or used by the Company over the past 5 years.		
XII.3 Engagement letters	Copies of contracts, agreements or engagement letters with investment bankers, finders, business brokers or other financial advisers pursuant to any contemplated financial transaction over the past 5 years.		

Section XIII. Imports & Exports

Item	Description	Comment	Received?
XIII.1 Imports	A description of the Company's major imports, the import process, and dealings with the US Customs Service		
XIII.2 Exports	A description of the Company's major exports and the export process. Include a detailed schedule of the Company's exports (both products and services), along with the annual amount of revenue derived from each export and the country to which the product or service was exported.		

| XIII.3 FCPA | A description of the Company's procedures and controls for complying with the Foreign Corrupt Practices Act. Include a detailed schedule of all sales representatives, commission agents, dealers and consultants dealing with foreign companies or agencies on the Company's behalf. | | |

Section XIV. Products & Services

Item	Description	Comment	Received?
XIV.1 Product and service lines	A detailed schedule of all existing products and services offered by the Company.		
XIV.2 Complaints	A detailed schedule of any complaints, warranty claims or litigation related to products or services offered by the Company.		
XIV.3 Internal reports	Copies of any tests, evaluations, studies, surveys and other internal reports related to existing or contemplates products and services.		

Section XV. Customer Information

Item	Description	Comment	Received?
XV.1 Customer list	A detailed schedule of the Company's customers, along with annual sales to each customer over the past 5 years.		
XV.2 Terms and conditions	A description of the Company's standard sales terms and conditions.		
XV.3 Market activities	Description of all marketing research, campaigns, plans, programs, budget and materials.		
XV.4 Competitors	A list of the Company's 10 most significant competitors.		

Section XVI. Other			
Item	**Description**	**Comment**	**Received?**
XVI.1 Professionals	A detailed schedule of all law firms, accounting firms, consulting firms and other professionals engaged by the Company over the past 5 years.		
XVI.2 Licenses and permits	Copies of all licenses, permits or consents held by the Company.		
XVI.3 Press releases	Copies of all press releases issued by the Company over the past 5 years.		
XVI.4 Insurance policies	Copies of all insurance policies, whether by third parties or self insured.		
XVI.5 Claims	A detailed schedule of the Company's insurance claims history over the past 5 years.		
XVI.6 Other significant matters	Any other document or information that may be significant to the Company or its operations.		

Manufacturas Lizard*

The following case study illustrates the various issues that need to be taken into account during an acquisition process envisaging the merger between two companies. It refers in particular to the formal aspects of the due diligence and the agreements between the parties, and encourages a broad discussion of the main factors that need to be negotiated in order to set a price and form of payment, bearing in mind the possible accounting adjustments and possible tax contingencies. This case has been used in courses on valuing companies and leveraged buyouts both as a part of the MBA programme and in the Master in Finance. It has also been used in specialist seminars. The case study offers an excellent opportunity to analyse the various different components of the valuation process, with special emphasis on the generation of value through the anticipated synergies. It also allows for discussion on economic value within the context of a negotiation process between the buyer and the seller.

In early June 2011, Julio Hernández, general manager of the company Plásticos Reales S.A. (PERESA), decided that he had better devote most of his time over the next few days to preparing for an upcoming meeting. This was due to take place on the 15th and would be an opportunity for PERESA to make a counter-offer for the purchase of Manufacturas Lizard S.A. by proposing a revised price for the company.

As the leader of PERESA's negotiating team, Mr Hernández was aware that buying Lizard potentially represented a unique opportunity for the company's growth strategy, and that the next meeting could be decisive to completing the transaction.

However, one of the vendor company's negotiating team had made a comment that summed up the state of the negotiations at that point:

"The negotiations we began four months ago are at a critical point right now. Everything went as smooth as silk, until we broached the *minor detail* of the price."

Some background information about Manufacturas Lizard, S.A.

Manufacturas Lizard S.A. (MALISA) was a family firm founded in 1975 by Mr José Castro and was devoted to the production of plaster and gypsum for use as building materials. Plaster and gypsum are composite materials mainly consisting of semihydrate and anhydrate calcium sulphate. They are obtained by processing chalk and have the property that after mixing with water they harden on contact with air as a result of crystallisation of the hydrated calcium sulphate.

MALISA had its headquarters in Sabanagrande, a town near Barranquilla, in the north of Colombia. Although ownership of the company was spread among various members of the Castro family, the control and management of the company was in the hands of Santiago Castro, the founder's son, who held the position of general manager.

The company sold its production through general (non-specialist) building materials distributors. In 2011, the gypsum and plaster sector for the construction industry in Colombia was highly fragmented, with very few exclusive distribution agreements.

MALISA's market was primarily centred on the north of Colombia, where it had a market share of close to 50%. The company did not have a nationwide presence. Its main competitor was another local producer, Materiales de Construcción y Cementos (MCC), which was present throughout the country and accounted for the remaining 50% of the market in the north.

Prices in the north-Colombian plaster market were significantly higher than in the rest of the country, due to the strength of demand and the fact that production and marketing were very concentrated.

In late 2010, Santiago Castro felt that MALISA's position was untenable in the medium to long term. In his opinion, the company lacked the financial resources necessary to compete with MCC over the long term, as the competitive advantages it currently enjoyed would not last forever. One possible solution would be for a financial partner to put up the resources necessary to develop the company, which had reserves of calcium sulphate that were excellent on account of their purity, size and location.

Moreover, Mr. Castro was aware that multinational firms interested in expanding in Latin America might have the company in their sights.

Starting the negotiations

One of these multinational firms was Plásticos Reales, S.A. (PERESA), a Spanish firm with a strategy of growth in new Latin American countries. Its general manager was Julio Hernández. Annex 1 gives audited accounting information about the company.

In 2010, PERESA's corporate development team studied the state of the market in Colombia, and suggested that the possible acquisition of Lizard was a perfect match for PERESA's strategic goals. In early 2011, Mr Hernández was entrusted with the task of starting conversations with MALISA's management with a view to negotiating a possible acquisition. The initial contacts took place in February and March, and the negotiations between the companies proceeded in an atmosphere of mutual interest and cooperation. In early March 2011 the two companies agreed to start the due diligence process.[1]

By the end of March 2011, the negotiations had reached a point at which there was a general agreement about the terms of the acquisition, as regards the operational aspects and future plans. The confidentiality agreements and a first letter of intent were therefore signed.[2] However, the always-delicate issues of the price and form of payment remained to be discussed.

A valuation of Manufacturas Lizard (MALISA)

In order to focus discussion towards a possible agreement on the price, both parties decided to make their own valuation of MALISA. To enable the purchaser (PERESA) to make its valuation, MALISA provided the accounting information listed in Annexure 2.

Based on this information, the CEO of the vendor company, Mr Castro, proposed a value for MALISA based on its book value plus a premium. For the vendor's part, the upper and lower limits for the negotiations were in the range of 1.20 and 1.46 US dollars per share, as shown in Annexure 3.

Table 1: Summary of the valuations of MALISA proposed by the management of Lizard

Accounting Value of Equity (thousands of US dollars)	6.266
Lower premium on accounting value	15%
Lower value of MALISA´s Equity (thousands of US dollars)	7.206
Lower price of MALISA´s share (US dollars)	1.20
Ratio E/EBITDA at lower price	2.91
Higher premium on accounting value	40%
Higher value of MALISA´s Equity (thousands of US dollars)	8.772
Higher price of MALISA´s share (US dollars)	1.46
Ratio E/EBITDA at higher price	3.54

1. The process of due diligence is embarked upon when the parties have agreed the general terms of the merger and it is a preliminary step before signing and exchanging contracts. It involves an investigation which may be defined as a search for information by the purchasing company so as to analyse the risks affecting the company it wishes to buy. It starts at the same time as the formal negotiations. This process does not normally begin until the more general principles and at least the foundations of the transaction have been agreed by the parties, or in some cases, when a serious offer is made. See: "Fusiones y Adquisiones en la práctica" García Estévez, P. and López Lubián, F. Delta Publicaciones. Madrid 2011.

2. After the initial contact between the parties, and before the due diligence is undertaken, the parties agree the more general terms and the foundations of the transaction. When a candidate is identified, a Memorandum of Understanding is signed. The Memorandum of Understanding is a type of non-binding agreement which sets out the undertakings which may later form the basis of the contractual agreement. In it, an undertaking is declared, or an intention stated to start or continue negotiations which may lead to a final agreement on the purchase. Memoranda of Understanding share some features with written contracts but in general, are not entirely binding on the parties. Many, however, contain binding clauses, such as the non-disclosure of the agreements, a good-faith clause, or a willingness to promise exclusive negotiating rights. The importance of this document lies in the fact that it establishes the pacts that may have been reached so far and delimits the set of points on which a satisfactory agreement has to be reached. It may propose an approximate sum to be paid for the shares or assets of the company being sold. See: "Fusiones y Adquisiones en la práctica" García Estévez, P. and López Lubián, F. Delta Publicaciones. Madrid, 2011

In Mr. Castro's opinion, as the representative of the vendor, this valuation for MALISA was entirely reasonable as the market was paying an average of 3 times EBITDA in similar operations (see Annexure 1).

Although Mr. Hernández understood the reasoning behind the way the vendor had set the offered price, he was not convinced by the method. On his view, it would make more sense to try to negotiate the maximum and minimum prices thresholds based on the company's expectations and risks, and not just on the book value of its assets.

The audit results

As part of the due diligence process, PERESA ordered an audit on the unaudited financial statements supplied by MALISA. In late May, the international audit firm in charge of the audit delivered a report in which it suggested a series of adjustments should be made to the information initially submitted by MALISA.

Table 2 shows the proposed adjustments related to the Accumulated Profit and Loss Account for the period 2008-10.

If all these adjustments were included in P&L, the accumulated result of MALISA for the period 2008-10 would be substantially different (see Annexure 2). Moreover, these new earnings did not include possible tax contingencies that might arise from these adjustments. Obviously, changes were also made to the Balance Sheet as at 31 December 2010.

Table 3 summarizes the possible tax contingencies not included in the proposed adjustments.

Table 2: Adjustments to MALISA's profit and loss accounts, period 2008-10
Figures in thousands of US dollars

	EFFECT IN EARNINGS
Adjustment in Cost of Sales due to non accounted purchases	-445
Adjustment in Expenses	6.790
Adjustment in Cost of Sales due to VAT accounted as a cost	2.626
Adjustment in Expenses due to VAT accounted as an expense	1.126
Adjustment in Cost of Sales due to overvaluing inventories	-561
Adjustment in Sales for bad debts	-1.760
Adjustment in EPS	-2.675
Adjustment in Expenses due to non accounted rent	-1.025
Adjustment in Expenses due to capitalized investments	3.220
Total effect in Operating Earnings	7.295

EPS = Employee Profit Sharing. Estimated at 10% of the earnings before taxes and EPS.

Table 3: Summary of possible tax contingencies affecting Lizard, as at 31-12-2010 (Figures in thousands of US dollars)

CONCEPT	AMOUNT	INTEREST EXPENSES	FINES	TOTAL
Income tax	10,000	500	2,000	12,500
Value-Added tax	1,000	250	100	1,350
Employee profit sharing (EPS)	200	100	32	332
Payroll tax	200	100	150	450
Other fines	0	0	368	368
Totals	11,400	950	2,650	15,000

A new valuation of MALISA

In the light of the information provided by the auditors, Mr Hernández felt that a correct valuation of MALISA should be based on these audited financial statements, as in his opinion, they gave a better picture of the operational situation of the company.

In order to negotiate the maximum and minimum price thresholds, Mr Hernández thought that both parts should reach an agreement on the value of the company in a continuity scenario (minimum price), and the value of the company in a scenario including the main synergies that would derive from the acquisition process (maximum price).

After his management team analyzed MALISA's earnings after adjustments, Mr Hernández considered that the maximum and minimum prices could be summarized in the assumptions given in Annexure 4.

Counter offer and negotiations with MALISA

As mentioned, the date for the meeting with MALISA to discuss and negotiate PERESA's counter offer was set for 15 June 2011. Mr Hernández was aware of the importance of this meeting in order to reach an agreement on the acquisition of MALISA. In his experience, to achieve a good outcome from this sort of meetings it was important to go well prepared (with homework done in advance) and pursue a clear negotiating strategy.

To this end, he drew up a list of the key points that needed to be addressed in order to conclude the transaction successfully:

Independently on the final price, both PERESA and MALISA (Lizard) are extremely interested in the operation. Over the course of the negotiations, the level of mutual understanding has been high, and everything points to a promising future for this acquisition.

The seller (MALISA, and more specifically Mr Castro) has in mind a minimum price of around seven million dollars, based on a multiple of EBITDA and a premium on the net book value. The offer should be made in these terms.

The results of the audit have already been implicitly accepted by the seller, as mentioned in the memorandum of understanding signed in March.

In order to facilitate negotiations, it will be a good idea to differentiate the proposed adjustments from the estimated tax contingencies. Including the former is crucial to obtaining a clear idea of the operational situation of the company. The tax contingencies can be discussed and dealt with separately.

If the maximum and minimum values are analyzed, based on the expected future cash flows provided by PERESA, what might seller's (Lizard) response be? What reasonable arguments can it provide to increase the value?

Annexure 1
Accounting information about PERESA audited figures.
In thousands of US dollars

1.   Profit and Loss (P/L) Account. Fiscal Year 2010

Net sales	50.125
Cost of Sales	-28.520
Gross Margin	21.605
Operating Expenses	-18.547
Operating Income	3.058
Other Income/Expenses	-200
EBIT	2.858
Taxes	-857
Net Income	2.001

2.   Balance sheet at the end of 31-12-2010

ASSETS		LIABILITIES	
Current Assets		Current Liabilities	
Cash in hands	200		
Account Receivables	5.000	Account Payables	3.500
Inventories	2.000	Deferred Taxes	411
Prepaid Taxes	511	Other Current Liabilities	2.000
Other Current Assets	100		
Total Current Assets	7.811		
Gross Fixed Assets	18.200		
Accumulated Depreciation	-11.000	Equity	7.100
Net Fixed Assets	7.200		
Total Assets	15.011	Total Liab + Equity	15.011

Annexure 2
Historical and account information about MALISA
Provided by the management of Lizard. Unaudited figures. In thousands of US dollars

1. P&L Accounts

YEARS	2008		2009		2010		TOTAL 2008-10	
Net sales	32.300		32.244		31.275		95.819	
Cost of Sales	-18.773	-58%	-18.741	-58%	-18.516	-59%	-56.030	-58%
Gross Margin	13.527	42%	13.503	42%	12.759	41%	39.789	42%
Operating Expenses	-10.666	-33%	-12.639	-39%	-10.973	-35%	-34.278	-36%
Operating Income	2.861	9%	864	3%	1.787	6%	5.512	6%
Other Income/ Expenses	534	2%	105	0%	0	0%	639	1%
EBIT	3.395	11%	969	3%	1.787	6%	6.151	6%
Taxes	-852	-3%	-538	-2%	-536	-2%	-1.926	-2%
EPS	-193	-1%	0	0%	0	0%	-193	0%
Net Income	2.350	7%	431	1%	1.251	4%	4.032	4%

Variation in EBITDA (earnings before interest, tax, depreciation and amortization):

YEARS	2008		2009		2010		TOTAL 2008-10
Net sales	32.300	100%	32.244	100%	31.275	100%	95.819
Operating Earnings	2.861	9%	864	3%	1.787	6%	5.512
Depreciation & Amort Exp	646	2%	645	2%	626	2%	1.916
EBITDA	3.507	11%	1.509	5%	2.412	8%	7.428
EBITDA average							2.476

E/EBITDA ratio paid in recent transactions:

2. Balance sheet at the end of 31-12-2010

ASSETS		LIABILITIES	
Current Assets		Current Liabilities	
Cash in hands	3.601		
Account Receivables	4.729	Account Payables	4.425
Inventories	1.374	Deferred Taxes	484
Prepaid Taxes	511	Other Current Liabilities	2.888
Other Current Assets	51		
Total Current Assets	10.266		
Gross Fixed Assets	9.797		
Accumulated Depreciation	-6.000	Equity	6.266
Net Fixed Assets	3.797		
Total Assets	14.063	Total Liab + Equity	14.063

Note: Number of shares: 6,000

Annexure 3: P&L account
including adjustments proposed by the auditors and excluding possible tax contingencies
Figures in thousands of US dollars

	Initial 2008-10	Purchases Adjust	Dividends Adjust	VAT Adjust	Invent Adjust	Bad Debts Adjust	EPS Adjust	Cap Invest Adjust	Rent Adjust	P&L after Adjust	
Net sales	95,819					-1,760				94059	
Cost of Sales	-56,030	-445		2,626	-561					-54,420	-58%
Gross Margin	39,789									39,649	42%
Operating Expenses	-34,278		6,790	1,126				3,220	-1,025	-24,167	-26%
Operating Earnings	5,512									15,482	16%
Other Income/ Expenses	639									639	1%
EBIT	6,151									16,121	17%
Taxes	-1,926									-1,926	-2%
EPS	-193						-2,675			-2,868	-3%
Net Earnings	4,032									11,327	12%
Extra or Tax Adj										-15,000	-16%
Net income after Adj										-3673	-4%

Estimated Balance Sheet at the end of 31-12-2010, including proposed adjustments

	Initial Balance	Bad Debt Adjust	Invent Adjust	EPS Adjust	Fixed Ass Adjust	Rent Adjust	Other Adjust	Balance after Adjust
ASSETS								
Current Assets								
Cash in hands	3.601			-2.675				926
Account Receivables	4.729	-1.760						2.969
Inventories	1.374		-561					813
Prepaid Taxes	511							511
Other Current Assets	51						3.307	3.358
Total Current Assets	10.266							8.577
Gross Fixed Assets	9.797				3.220			13.017
		-6.000						-6.000
Net Fixed Assets	3.797							7.017
Total Assets	14.063							15.594
LIABILITIES								
Current Liabilities								
Account Payables	4.425							4.425
Deferred Taxes	484							484
Other Current Liabilities	2.888					1.025		3.913
Total Current Liabilities	7.797							8.822
Equity	6.266	-1.760	-561	-2.675	3.220	-1.025	3.307	6.772
Total Liab + Equity	14.063							15.594

EBIT	16.121
Taxes (30%)	-4.836
Net Earnings before EPS	11.284
EPS (10% debt & EPS)	-1.612
Net Earnings after EPS	9.672
Depreciation	1.916
Operational FCF	11.589
Operational FCF as % Sales	12%

Scenarios for the valuation of MALISA minimum price scenario (Continuity)

Sales: year-on-year increase in sales of 5%.

FCF from Operations: 12% of each year's sales (see Annex 2). Amortization/ depreciation remains stable at 2% of sales.

FCF from operational working capital: Working capital will increase by the same percentage as sales.

FCF from investments in fixed assets: An annual investment in maintenance will be needed that is equal to the amortization/depreciation charges. In addition, Lizard will need new investments for a value of 2,000 in year 1. These investments will be maintained over the following years, growing by 5% each year.

Horizon of analysis: 5 years. The terminal value in the final year is estimated as perpetuity with a growth of 3%.

In order to estimate WACC it is assumed that:

The current capital structure does not change.

$K_d = 5\%$

$R_f = 4\%$

$PM = 4\%$

Beta e,u = 1.2

There is a country risk premium of 200 basis points.

The tax rate is 30%.

Maximum price scenario (including Synergies)

The synergies PERESA will obtain through its purchase of MALISA may be summarized by the following points:

FCF from Operations becomes 13% as of the second year

FCF from operational working capital: The working capital would increase by 4% as of the third year.

These improvements rest on three basic points:

The possibility of introducing new products and improving the mix of the existing ones. Possible improvements in production processes, through enhancements in quality and a reduction in costs.

Bolstering of the sales and marketing area, which would enable access to new customers and markets, and it would also consider exports.

Suggested questions for the discussion and answers

1. **What is your view on the operation described in the case study? Does it make sense? Why?**

   The case study describes a typical acquisition of one company by another with a view to their subsequent merger. The operation makes sense insofar as the two parties have an interest in its going ahead.

   The interest for the target company (MALISA) may be summarised by the following points:

   a) The company is currently very profitable, but it has a business model and strategy, which do not appear to be sustainable over the medium-to-long term.

   b) It needs financial resources in order to sustain its competitive position.

   c) It is at an optimum moment at which to obtain a good selling price.

   The interest for the buyer (PERESA) lies mainly in the following points:

   a) The purchase of MALISA fits in perfectly with its strategy of overseas growth.

   b) PERESA has resources with which to leverage the purchase.

   c) PERESA's management of operations can yield synergies in the acquired company.

2. **What do you think of the adjustments proposed by the auditors? Do they seem reasonable? Why?**

   The adjustments appear to be reasonable as they relate to practices that are widespread among family-owned businesses.

   These are actions such as:

   1) Concealed dividends paid as general expenses.

   2) Lack of provisions for possible bad debts.

   3) Capitalization of Fixed asset investments

   4) Overvaluation of inventories.

   5) EPS (employee profit sharing) not properly provisioned.

   6) Use of fixed assets by the family free of charge.

   7) Incorrect accounting for VAT.

3. **What is your opinion on the possible tax contingencies suggested by the auditors? Are they reasonable? Why? How should they be taken into account in the negotiations?**

   The tax contingencies that derive from the adjustments always represent the maximum risk, in which the total amount becomes payable, with interest and the applicable penalties. Obviously, this is a sum that needs to be covered and must be negotiated.

In the answer to the following question, a way of covering contingencies of this type is discussed.

4. **Imagine you are on Mr Hernández's team: estimate the minimum and maximum price for MALISA based on the criteria described in the case. What would your negotiating strategy be at the meeting on 15 June?**

Bearing in mind that an initial price of between 1.20 and 1.46 US dollars per share already exists, the counter-offer should explain in detail the origin of the different prices and give convincing reasons for accepting them.

Following the assumptions set out in Annex 3, we can estimate the maximum and minimum values (figures in thousands of US dollars).

a) Minimum value (business as usual)

Estimated free cash flow (FCF):

Years		1	2	3	4	5
Sales		32.839	34.481	36.205	38.015	39.916
Operational FCF		3.972	4.17	4.379	4.598	4.828
Evolution of NCA::						
Present balance	-245	-258	-271	-284	-298	-313
Increase of 5%	-12	12	13	14	14	15
Capital expenditures:						
Maintenance		-657	-690	-724	-760	-798
New investments		-2	-2.1	-2.205	-2.315	-2.431
Total		-2.657	-2.79	-2.929	-3.076	-3.229
FCF		1.327	1.394	1.463	1.536	1.613
TV						21.304
Total FCF to discount						22.917

Associated WACC

D	0%	R_f	4%
E	100%	MP	4%
		Beta u	1.2
K_d	5%	Beta l	1.2
K_e	11%	CRP	2%
T	30%	K_e	10,8%
WACC	10.8%		

As a result, discounting the FCF at this WACC, we obtain the estimated value of the company and that of its equity:

Enterprise Value (EV)	18.151
Adjustments:	
Increase in E	506
Debt	0
Equity at Econ Value	18.657
Ratio E/EBITDA (no fiscal contingencies)	3.11 times
Estimated price of share	3.11

b) Maximum value (exploiting synergies)

Estimated free cash flow:

Years		1	2	3	4	5
Sales		32.839	34.481	36.205	38.015	39.916
Operational FC		3.972	4.482	4.707	4.942	5.189
Evolution of NCA:						
Present balance	-245					
Increase of 5%	-12	12	13	13	14	14
Capital expenditures:						
Maintenance		-657	-690	-724	-760	-798
New investments		-2.000	-2.100	-2.205	-2.315	-2.431
		-2.657	-2.79	-2.929	-3.076	-3.229
FCF		1.327	1.706	1.791	1.880	1.974
TV						26.070
Total FCF to discount		1.327	1.706	1.791	1.880	26.070
		1.327	1.706	1.791	1.880	28.044

In this scenario the WACC remains at 10.8%. Discounting the FCF at this WACC, we obtain the estimated value of the company and of its equity:

Enterprise Value (EV)	21.945
Adjustments:	
Increase in E	506
Debt	0
Equity at Econ Value	22.451
Ratio E/EBITDA (no fiscal contingencies)	3,74 times
Estimated price of share	3.74

Of course, the tax contingencies of around 15 million must be covered by the vendor.

There are several ways this can be done.

One option is as follows:

1) PERESA buys the net assets of MALISA, valued, for example at 15,000. It pays with a rights issue increasing PERESA's capital, which is subscribed by the shareholders of MALISA.

2) Although the contingencies remain in the empty shell of MALISA, if they arise, they can affect the asset sale transaction. Therefore, MALISA's shareholders need to establish a guarantee for the total amount of the possible cover in an escrow account, or in the form of a bond payable on first demand.

5. **Imagine you are on Mr Castro's team. Given the valuation put forward by Mr Hernández, what arguments would you use in order to negotiate a higher price? What would your negotiating strategy be at the meeting on 15 June?**

The summary of the prices offered so far is as follows (in dollars per share):

	MINIMUM PRICE	MAXIMUM PRICE
Seller's initial offer:	1.20	1.46
Buyer's counter offer:		
New price	3.11	3.74
Fiscal contingencies	2.50	2.50
New price including fiscal contingencies	0.61	1.24

Apart from the tax contingencies, the adjusted price estimated by the discounted cash flows may be greater, as the evaluation above excludes the increase in value from possible excess cash and the possible use of debt in the capital structure.

Therefore, as advisor to the seller, and accepting the assumptions included in the valuation offered by the buyer, the adjusted prices without tax contingencies may increase, depending on the level of debt and what the excess cash is considered to be.

Thus:

Value in the business-as-usual scenario (minimum) of MALISA, with a capital structure of 30% debt (figures in US dollars):

Years		1	2	3	4	5
Sales		32.839	34.481	36.205	38.015	39.916
Operating FCF		3.972	4.17	4.379	4.598	4.828
Evolution of NCA						
Present balance	-245	-258	-271	-284	-298	-313
		12	13	14	14	15
Capital expenditures:						
Maintenance		-657	-690	-724	-760	-798
New investments		-2.000	-2.100	-2.205	-2.315	-2.431
		-2.657	-2.79	-2.929	-3.076	-3.229
FCF		1.327	1.394	1.463	1.536	1.613
TV		1.327	1.394	1.463	1.536	23.57
Total FCF to discount						25.183

Nuevo WACC:

D	30%	R_f	4%
E	70%	MP	4%
		Beta u	1,2
K_d	5%	Beta l	1,7
K_e	13%	CRP	2%
t	30%	K_e	12.9%
WACC	10,1%		

Therefore:

Enterprise Value (EV)	20.103
Adjustments:	
Increase in E	506
Debt	0
Equity at Econ Value	20.609
Ratio E/EBITDA (no fiscal contingencies)	3.43
Estimated price of share	3.43

The share value, excluding tax contingencies, is now $3.43 (US).

The estimated share value in the scenario with synergies (maximum value) is $4.14 (excluding tax contingencies).

In other words, the counter offer from the seller, accepting the buyer's operating assumptions, but including the value generating capacity of the excess cash and the non-use of debt, would be:

	MINIMUM PRICE	MAXIMUM PRICE
Price with at 30% and excluding contingencies	3.43	4.14
with contingencies	0.93	1.64

The forecast range of prices for an agreement (excluding contingencies) could be situated between 2.50 and 4.00 dollars per share. And including contingencies between 0 and 1.5 dollars per share.

* **This case and its teaching notes have been prepared by Prof. Francisco López Lubián**, Business School C/ Castellón de la Plana, 8, 28006 Madrid,, Spain (Fco.Lubian@ie.edu). The author is deeply indebted to his contribution to this book.

Glossary

Acquisition Acquirer purchases a controlling financial interest in an acquiree and agrees to operate it as a majority owned or wholly owned subsidiary.

Acquisition method Required by FAS-141R and FAS-160 for consolidation of companies controlled by an acquirer; focuses on business fair value, not historical price paid to acquire a company.

Asset Spinoff The defending party identifies the assets most desirable to the raider. It then spins off the assets to one of its separate companies or sells them to a third party.

Bargain purchase Under the acquisition method, when business fair value is less than the fair value of net assets received; under the purchase method, when purchase price is less than the fair value of net assets acquired.

Book value Amount recorded on the accounting records, also referred to as "carrying value."

Business combinations (mergers and acquisitions) Legal joining of two or more companies into one economic entity.

Business fair value The sum of the fair value of the controlling interest and the fair value of the noncontrolling (minority) interest.

Capitalization The conversion of income into value. The capital structure of a business. The determination of an asset value based on expenditures.

Capitalization factor The inverse of a capitalization rate. For example, a capitalization rate of 25% is a capitalization factor of 4.0 (1.0/25%). Capitalization factors and capitalization rates are used interchangeably by appraisers.

Capitalization of earnings valuation method A valuation methodology that presumes the value of a business is generally determined by dividing its earnings by the investment rate of return the business should yield for investors.

Capitalization rate A divisor used to convert an income amount into a value equivalent. The rate used in the denominator of the capitalization of earnings method. Generally determined to be the rate of return expected for an investment, reduced by the growth expected for the investment. A key component of many valuations is the determination

173

of this rate.

Capital structure Usually, the percentage of the company's invested capital made up of interest bearing debt and equity. Possibly, the composition of the liabilities and equity side of the balance sheet. Possibly, values restated to fair market values.

Cash flow Cash income created by a company. Often defined as net cash flow or gross cash flow.

CDOs *See* corporate development officers (CDOs).

Conglomerate merger This occurs when two companies in unrelated industries combine, such as where an electronics company joins with an insurance company.

Consolidation With a consolidation, two or more companies combine to create a new company. None of the consolidation firms legally survive. For example, companies A and B give all their assets, liabilities, and stock to the new company, C, in return for C's stock, bonds, or cash.

Contingent consideration Amounts that may be paid at a future date by the acquirer based on whether certain conditions are met (e.g., earnings, stock price, or employee retention).

Control The ability (whether used or not) of the acquirer to make decisions about the manner in which the acquiree conducts business (e.g., pricing of products, dividends, use of technology, or interchange of management personnel).

Control premium Additional amount paid by the acquirer to gain a controlling financial interest in the acquiree.

Corporate development officers (CDOs) The heads of in-house merger and acquisition teams.

Cost, equity, and partial equity methods Alternative accounting methods used by a parent to account for its investment in its consolidated subsidiary on the parent's books.

Direct acquisition costs Costs incurred to complete the business combination (e.g., lawyer's and accountant's fees).

Discounted earnings valuation method A valuation methodology that presumes the value of a business or ownership holding is equivalent to the expected earnings anticipated for the company in future years. A conceptually sound methodology often dismissed as being too speculative to be valuable for fair market value appraisals.

Discount rate A rate of return used to convert a value in the future into a present value. The rate of return used to discount future values to present values in the discounted earnings valuation method.

Discretionary cash flow Cash flows of a business generally available for distributions to owners and for reinvestment.

Divestiture involves the partial or complete conversion, disposition and reallocation of people, money, inventories, plants, equipment and products.

Due diligence An investigation or audit of a potential investment. Due diligence serves to confirm all material facts in regards to a sale. Generally, due diligence refers to the care a reasonable person should take before entering in an agreement or transaction with another party.

Economic unit method for consolidation of noncontrolling interests Required by FAS-160 for consolidation of noncontrolling interests arising from acquisitions completed by acquirers having a fiscal year beginning after December 15, 2008.

Excess earnings valuation method A valuation method that presumes a company should be able to earn a predictable level of income based on its tangible assets. To the extent the company earns more than the predictable level of income, capitalized, the company is deemed to have intangible assets. Also referred to as the "formula" method, the IRS method, and the Treasury method.

Fair (market) value The price at which property would change hands between a willing buyer and a willing seller, in an arm's length transaction, when both parties have relevant knowledge of the facts, and neither is compelled to buy or sell. The definition of value for tax valuations and many others.

Golden parachute Management compensation arrangements that are triggered when there is a purchase of the business such as lump-sum benefits, employment agreements, and stock options. Recent examples are Greyhound and Hughes Tool.

Greenmail The target company buys back the stock accumulated by the raider, at a premium. Recent examples are Texaco, Walt Disney, and Goodyear.

Herfindahl-Hirshman Index (HHI) The sum of the squared market shares multiplied by 10,000 to eliminate the need for decimals. By squaring the market shares before adding them up, the index weights firms with high market shares more heavily. The value of the Herfindahl-Hirshman Index lies between 0 and 10,000. A value of 10,000 exists when a monopolist exists in the industry. A value of zero results when there are numerous infinitesimally small firms. The HHI is used by the Department of Justice to evaluate horizontal merges.

Holding company One whose sole purpose is to own the stock of other companies. In a tender offer, the buyer goes directly to the stockholders of the target business to tender (sell) their shares, typically for cash.

Horizontal merger This occurs when two companies in a similar business combine. An example is the combining of two airlines.

Goodwill Future economic benefits, obtained in a business combination, that are not attributable to separately recognized assets and liabilities of the acquiree.

Implied value Price paid to acquire a company divided by ownership percentage; used for the goodwill impairment test and the economic unit method of consolidating noncontrolling interests.

In process research and development costs Amounts expended by the acquiree for research and development costs prior to the date of acquisition, regardless of whether they are treated as an asset or expense on the acquiree books.

Intangible assets Gives the owner rights transferred by contract or other means.

Intercompany transactions Transactions that take place within the same economic entity, typically between a parent and a subsidiary.

Leveraged buyouts (LBO) refers to a very popular form of taxable transaction in which the purchase price is funded primarily by lenders rather than by the buyer.

Liquidation value The value of a business not as a going concern. Often, the accumulated value of a company's assets (less liabilities) presuming the assets are sold separately.

Merger In a merger, two or more companies are combined into one, where only the acquiring company retains its identity. Generally, the larger of the two companies is the acquirer.

Net assets Total assets minus total liabilities.

Noncontrolling interests (sometimes referred to as minority interests) Owner-ship associated with holders of less than 50% of the voting common shares of the acquiree.

PAC-MAN The defending company makes a counteroffer for the stock of the raiding company. Recent examples are American Brands and Bendix Corporation.

Parent company Acquirer, when the acquiree is operated as a subsidiary.

Parent company method for consolidation of noncontrolling interests Most prevalent method prior to the new consolidation standards for consolidation of noncontrolling interests—acquiree balance sheet accounts consolidated at 100% of book value þ (ownership percentage · [fair value - book value]); this method was viewed as a "hybrid method" between the economic unit method and the proportionate method.

Poison pill When a hostile bid is eminent, the targeted company takes out significant debt (or issues preferred stock) that makes the company unattractive to the hostile acquirer because of the high debt position.

Pooling of interests method Accounting method that is intended to reflect a "merger of equals"; acquiree book values (not fair values) are recorded in consolidation; there is no goodwill in a pooling (no longer available to acquisitions closed after June 30, 2001).

Preacquisition contingencies Uncertainties that arose prior to the date of the acquisition (e.g. lawsuits) that will be resolved after the acquisition closing date.

Price/earnings valuation method The valuation of a company or ownership interest in which a ratio determined by publicly traded stocks or sales of closely held businesses is used to value the subject business. For example, if the price/earnings ratio is determined to be 6.2, and the subject company's earnings are $100,000, the value of the company is estimated to be $620,000 ($100,000 times 6.2).

Proportionate method for consolidation of noncontrolling interests Acquiree assets and liabilities consolidated at fair value multiplied by the percentage of ownership; this method is no longer permissible for new acquisitions subject to FAS-160.

Purchase method Accounting method that focuses on the historical cost of the acquisition (e.g., price paid by the parent); acquiree assets and liabilities are recorded in consolidation at fair value (no longer available to acquisitions closed after December 15, 2008, where the acquirer's fiscal year-end begins on or after that date).

Recapitalization is a nontaxable exchange that is typically used to pass control of a corporation to new owners, frequently the younger generation.

Self-Tender After a hostile bid, the target company itself makes a counteroffer for its own shares. A recent example is Newmont Mining.

Statutory consolidation Both companies agree to merge with a newly formed company replacing the two previous companies.

Statutory merger Acquirer purchases net assets or stock of acquiree and dissolves the acquiree, bringing the net assets on to the acquirer books at fair value (acquisition method).

Stock issuance costs Costs to register securities issued in conjunction with a business combination (e.g., exchange fees, printing costs [prospectus]).

Subsidiary company Acquiree, when it is operated as a subsidiary of the parent.

Valuation The act or process of assigning a value to something. Generally synonymous with "appraisal."

Variable interest entity Entity where the primary beneficiary (generally, the sponsor) does not own shares but nonetheless maintains control through contractual agreement (sometimes referred to as a special purpose vehicle or special purpose entity).

Vertical merger This occurs when a company combines with a supplier or customer. An example is when a wholesaler combines with retailers.

White Knight The defending company finds a third party who is willing to pay a higher premium, typically with "friendlier" intentions than the raider. Recent examples are Gulf Oil Corp. (Chevron) and Sterling Drugs (Eastman Kodak).

Index

DATE DUE	RETURNED
NOV 27 2010	